HAROLD FALKNER

More than an Arts & Crafts Architect

HAROLD FALKNER

More than an Arts & Crafts Architect

Sam Osmond

PHILLIMORE

2003

Published by
PHILLIMORE & CO. LTD
Shopwyke Manor Barn, Chichester, West Sussex, England

ISBN 1 86077 253 6

Printed and bound in Great Britain by
BUTLER & TANNER LTD
London and Frome

Contents

List of Illustrations

Colour Plates (between pages 46 and 47)

Acknowledgements

In my research I have been helped by many people, for anyone who knows about Falkner feels that a book about him is needed. In particular I would like to thank George Baxter, Susan Farrow, and Michael Blower for their encouragement and their knowledge, which is much greater than my own.

I have also drawn on Nigel Temple's unrivalled expertise on the buildings of Farnham, and Denise Todd's special knowledge of Surrey Arts and Crafts, and been greatly helped by Chris Hellier in delving among the archives of the Museum of Farnham.

Susan Farrow was kind enough to read the first draft, and Nigel Temple the second, but any errors or omissions which remain are entirely mine. It was especially kind of David Watkin to take the time from his busy life to write the Foreword and make some further helpful suggestions.

My thanks also to the owners of Falkner houses, who have graciously opened their doors to me, and to all the individuals who have shared with me their personal memories of Falkner.

I am grateful to the Museum of Farnham for allowing me to reproduce many of Harold Falkner's drawings, to the estate agents of Farnham who have built up a special experience of Falkner houses, and to all those concerned who have allowed me to reproduce their pictures—especially Michael Blower for his sketches and Michael Clements for his colour photographs.

Harold Falkner's surviving family members, his great-nephew Hugh Falkner and his great-niece Diana Harrison (and their step-father Ronald Cooper who gave me a masterly family tree), have been good enough to share their childhood memories of Harold Falkner. I hope this book will convince them that he was a lot more than the funny old man whom they remember today.

Illustration Acknowledgements

Michael Clements, 40, I, III, IV, VII, IX-XI, XIII-XV; The Farnham Herald, 8, 56; Godalming Museum, VIII; Hamptons International, 24; John D Wood & Co., II; Letchworth Heritage Museum, 25; Hubert de Lisle, 14; Museum of Farnham, 1-5, 11-12, 15, 31, 37-8, 43-4, 46-54; RIBA, 29 (right); Jane Ridley, 29 (left); Nigel Temple, 37 (top); Lady Verney, 55; Peter Walmsley, V; Fred Warren, 42; Alan Windsor, 39, 41; Peter Wright for Lane Fox, VI, XII; Zwemmer Publishing, 9.

Foreword

Harold Falkner (1875-1963), the brilliant and 'maverick' architect, as Sam Osmond justly describes him in this stimulating monograph, takes his place in a group of beleaguered and heroic architects who resisted with varying degrees of success the destruction of memory, history, local associations, and traditional materials, which the International Modern Movement made its aim to bring about from the 1930s. Osmond's book is especially welcome because, despite the change of architectural mood which began in the 1980s, the Modernist orthodoxy against which Falkner heroically struggled is still far from over, as is shown by the continuing stranglehold of architects such as Lord Foster of Bankside and Lord Rogers of Riverside on the architectural scene at the beginning of the twenty-first century.

The world in which Falkner moved was dominated for many years by the architectural genius of his near contemporary, Sir Edwin Lutyens (1869-1944), whom Sam Osmond suggestively compares to Falkner. He points out that there were so many similarities in their early life, including their friendship with the influential gardener, Gertrude Jekyll, that it might have been expected that Falkner would have had the more successful career. Yet Lutyens achieved such success from the start of his career that he had attained an unchallengeable position by the time of the emergence of Modernism. Architects who were younger than Lutyens and therefore closer to Falkner in their resistance to Modernism included Sir Albert Richardson (1880-1964), Sir Clough Williams-Ellis (1883-1978), and Raymond Erith (1904-1973). The knighthoods achieved by two of these indicate a level of professional recognition that was never granted to Falkner. Osmond refers to the belief of Falkner's sometime partner, the architect Guy Maxwell Aylwin, that inheriting a large sum of money as a young man sapped Falkner of the energy required to achieve the success of which he was surely capable.

Yet external circumstances such as wealth tend to act on what they find in the individual human psyche, so that, for example, the creative flow of the architect, Sir John Soane, was not blocked by the inheritance in 1790, through his wife, of a fortune large enough to make it unnecessary for him to work again. If we can never fully understand the mystery of the artistic personality, we can celebrate with the help of Osmond's book the dozens of beautiful houses built by Falkner in and around Farnham, and, no less importantly, the example he set in repairing the damage which insensitive Victorian and twentieth-century alterations had effected in a historic town like Farnham. The crassly insensitive Modernist addition with which Sir Colin St John Wilson currently threatens to engulf Pallant House, the finest early Georgian house in Chichester, would, one hopes, be unthinkable in Farnham, thanks to the climate established by Falkner and his life-long friend and ally, Charles Borelli.

Osmond paints a full picture of the Arts and Crafts world from which Falkner sprang where William Morris, Philip Webb, and Norman Shaw, with their stress on domestic architecture, were the leading figures. He also conveys a vivid impression of the architectural debates which confronted him as a junior member of the Art Workers Guild. He goes on to explain the social and physical setting of Farnham and its changing class structure, pointing out how in Falkner's youth, and also today, it stands 'socially and geographically on the cusp between the commuter territory of outer London and the open farmlands of South West England.'

In this context, not the least part of this stimulating book is that Osmond shows the opposition Falkner met from the local author, George Sturt (1863-1927). Sturt's romantic approach to the lives of working people in nineteenth-century Surrey in books such as *Change in the Village* (1911), written under the pseudonym of George Bourne, led him to condemn what he saw as Falkner's reinvention of Farnham's past. For Sturt, the upper-middle-class domesticity for which Falkner catered destroyed the values of rural and cottage life. He thus complained of 'the multitude of villas going up—many of them by Harold Falkner' whom he saw as 'the evil genius of this countryside ... [in] his tasteless replacement of what was once the beautiful tree-lined gorse-covered Vicarage Hill'. In his thoughtful and well-balanced book, Osmond does not ignore the ill-disciplined nature of the nine houses which Falkner built in Dippenhall where he refused to abide by building regulations but integrated redundant farm buildings into a kind of *Lord of the Rings* earthiness.

Having spent my boyhood in Farnham in the 1950s and early 1960s, it was a pleasure as well as an honour to be invited to contribute a Foreword to so beautiful and distinguished a book. Farnham, and therefore Falkner's achievement, played a major role in my architectural education, especially in an urban fabric. Seeing the rape of East Street and South Street in the early '60s helped make me conscious of the threat to urban values which Modernism represented. I wrote my Ph.D. thesis in architectural history at Cambridge in the late 1960s as a pupil of Sir Nikolaus Pevsner who was, ironically, a ceaseless promoter of what I increasingly saw as the destructive and anti-historical forces of Modernism in architecture. It was thus fascinating to read in Osmond's book a letter which Falkner wrote to Pevsner at the end of his life in which he complained that, 'you and your fellow journalists are delighted to get away from something [the practice of traditional architecture] which takes a lot of understanding and even experience ... in the hope of finding something new. For thirty years you have been looking and have found nothing.' Astonishingly, Pevsner refused to mention Lutyens, arguably the greatest British architect since

Wren, in any of the many editions of his hugely influential *Outline of European Architecture* (1st edn 1942).

The Surrey volume of Pevsner's celebrated 'Buildings of England' series (1962, 2nd edn 1971) records that Farnham is 'generally ranked as one of the best Georgian towns in England', but complains that this 'is over-praise', partly because the town contains 'a depressing amount of Neo-Georgian.' As a result 'preservation has become stultification, so that there are now streets … where there are more Neo-Georgian houses than true Georgian ones.' It would be interesting to know what streets he had in mind. In the same book, Falkner's Farnham Town Hall of 1930-5 is dismissed as 'Neo-Georgian, inevitably, and rather pedestrian.' Yet Pevsner and his fellow Modernist propagandists never questioned the use of previous models in past centuries, reserving their objection to this practice in the 20th century. Palladio, for example, has been praised as the most imitated architect in history, with neo-Palladianism featuring continuously in architecture from even before his death in 1580. Yet Pevsner condemned all traditional design in the 20th century because the birth of 'modern man' called for total modernity in all things. However, no-one dismisses the great eighteenth-century country houses such as Houghton Hall or Holkham Hall in Norfolk as 'pedestrian' because they derive inspiration from Palladio. Sam Osmond aptly quotes Falkner as 'expostulating that he did not build "mock-Georgian" any more than he baked a "mock" apple pie when he used a tried and tested recipe.'

To call Farnham Town Hall 'neo-Georgian' and 'pedestrian' is to be blind to features such as its arcade with its subtle echoes of Quattrocento Florence, and to ignore the way in which it was far more sympathetic to Farnham than the Victorian Town Hall and Corn Exchange in white brick with red brick dressings which it replaced. Sam Osmond draws an appropriate parallel in this case with the recreation of Colonial Williamsburg in Virginia where the damage done to this icon of American Georgian architecture was patiently repaired from 1927 to 1960 in a process akin to that of a surgeon. Also, just as Falkner's Town Hall is not a Town Hall but has always had an entirely commercial function, so the newly rebuilt Governor's Palace in Williamsburg is, of course, not a Governor's Palace at all: it is, nonetheless, a monument of great resonance, sympathetic to its setting. The restricting Modernist doctrine that architecture must somehow be 'truthful' underplays the role which myth and fiction can play in architecture.

However, Falkner has found in Sam Osmond the ideal biographer for he not only describes his buildings but also quotes extensively from the writings in which he explained the theory underpinning his hostility to Modernism. Osmond's sympathetic yet always scholarly approach, based on full documentary research and providing the reader with a select bibliography, establishes and illustrates for the first time his extensive and varied output, ranging from 'Country mansion to council house, shop front to Town Hall, suburban house to factory.' He calculates that Falkner was responsible for about 115 buildings in Farnham and its neighbourhood which are recorded in a full list at the end of the book.

In a lecture at the Farnham Museum in 1994 the excellent architect Roderick Gradidge (1929-2000) provocatively claimed that there is nowhere else in the world, with the possible exception of the area round Vicenza where Palladio's villas are to be found, which can boast such a concentration of fine architecture as the neighbourhood of Farnham and Godalming. In his enchanting book, *Dream Houses: The Edwardian Ideal* (1980), Gradidge had already hailed Harold Falkner as 'that great Farnham original': there could be no happier description.

DAVID WATKIN
Professor of the History of Architecture
at the University of Cambridge

Introduction

One of the many surprising things about Harold Falkner is that no-one has written a book about him before. Here is an architect who had his drawings selected for the Royal Academy six times before he was 31, and by the age of 40, when most architects today have built little, had built 25 houses and commercial buildings and undertaken a major reconstruction of a 16th-century building. In the course of a long career he had over ninety articles or sketches published in the architectural press, built about eighty houses and thirty commercial buildings, and managed to turn his home town of Farnham into 'England's Williamsburg'. On his death Nikolaus Pevsner, doyen of architectural historians and opposed to most of Falkner's views, wrote his obituary for the *Architectural Review*. Five years after his death he was rediscovered by the *Architectural Review* as an architect of genius. Subsequently he has been the subject of five university dissertations, and featured largely in two books on architectural history and the first non-family biography of Gertrude Jekyll.

Why then, is he not better known outside Farnham? Part of the reason is that he lacked a burning ambition to take the national stage. He lacked the spur—a wife, a need for money or power, a desire to escape—to drive him beyond what fell effortlessly into his lap.

The contrast with Edwin Lutyens, who was just six years older, is instructive. Both boys grew up in the same corner of south-west Surrey and built their first buildings in or near Farnham. They had the same sort of architectural education—art school, working with a builder, and a couple of years with a famous London architectural practice. Each of them decided to set up his own business at the age of 20, and shortly afterwards became a friend of Gertrude Jekyll who lived not far away. Yet Lutyens had the burning ambition to be a national figure, and escape his father's slide into penury. Early on he took steps to achieve this—moving his office to London, cultivating friendships with Gertrude Jekyll's rich clients, marrying the daughter of an earl, and getting himself invited to country-house parties where he might meet new clients. Falkner did none of these things; he was content to stay in Farnham and never married. His ambition was more that of a medieval craftsman in the tradition of Ruskin: to do good craft work with his own hands and his own design.

In its larger dimension his ambition never really extended beyond trying to make his town of Farnham more architecturally interesting, with an 18th century bias. He formed an alliance with his old school-friend Charles Borelli, and for forty years nothing got built or demolished in the town that did not have their approval. The result has been a remarkable success, in the view of both its citizens and those from outside who value old English towns.

Like Lutyens, Falkner had developed his architectural thinking in the surroundings of the late 19th century—vernacular farmhouses, the Arts and Crafts movement, and the neo-Georgian style of his mentor Reginald Blomfield. He never deviated from these roots, though a more ambitious man might have tried to go along with the Modern Movement which swept across Europe.

This was the second reason which prevented him from achieving the national fame which his talents deserved. From its origins in 1920s Germany, the Modern Movement came to dominate all architectural thought in Europe and the USA. It rejected traditional materials, individual choice, any form of decoration, and the whole idea of architectural history. The Movement was dictatorial and intolerant, but surprisingly successful in imposing its ideas, and few architects of note could survive outside it.

Falkner became a maverick. He had no intention of subscribing to a movement which preached so many principles which ran counter to his values, and he was not shy about saying so. As a result he was excluded from *The Architectural Review*, for which he had been a regular contributor up to 1920. From 1906 to 1920 the Editor was Mervyn Macartney, an authority on Queen Anne and early Georgian buildings. From 1927 it was edited by the hard-line modernist Hubert Hastings, later abetted by Philip Morton Shand, friend of Gropius and Le Corbusier. They published nothing more about him until his obituary.

Being a maverick, Falkner never joined his old friend Goodhart-Rendel or his old mentor, Reginald Blomfield, in trying to stem the tide of Modernism. He contented himself with lobbing grenades from the security of his Farnham practice. He conducted a rumbustious debate in *The Architects' Journal* (then, as now, less authoritarian than *The Architectural Review*) with Professor Charles Reilly, head of the large architecture school at Liverpool, about the disadvantages of modern materials and the relevance of architectural history. In his execrable typing he corresponded with Nikolaus Pevsner over his claim that the Arts and Crafts movement could be viewed as Pioneers of the Modern Movement. He resigned from the Royal Institute of British Architects when they sponsored an exhibition about the Bauhaus. What Falkner had to say was deeply unfashionable at the time, yet within a few years of his death the first doubts about Modernism were expressed among the architectural establishment by Aldo Rossi and Robert Venturi, and a few years later, in a more sweeping form, by Peter Blake. Today Falkner's views sound, as he intended, very like a voice of common sense.

Doubtless he enjoyed his debate, and so did the readers of *The Architects' Journal*, but in fact by 1933 his architectural priorities were really elsewhere. In his last thirty years of work he regressed to become what he had always wanted to be—a man who put together buildings so steeped in the vernacular tradition that it was difficult to say exactly when they were built. The layout might look as if the building had grown haphazardly over centuries. His taste for incorporating some older building materials, which he had always liked to do, grew into a drive to incorporate whole barns which were genuinely old. The carving of the brickwork, stone or timber was done by hand—very often by Falkner himself, if he had not recycled it from elsewhere. In Falkner's last works we go the full circle back to the Ruskinian ideal of the medieval master mason, in a way which other Arts and Crafts architects had intended to achieve but few managed, with the possible exception of Ernest Gimson and Detmar Blow (although even for them it was not a phase which could be sustained).

Looking back on his work, one is surprised at his versatility since it comprised an astonishing variety from council house to country mansion, shop-front to Town Hall, suburban house to factory. In each case he managed to build in some link with the past. This was not a matter of constructing replicas, but buildings which had real antique touches—a doorway, a rainwater hopper, a chimney-piece, a newel post. He was equally versatile, and sensitive to history, when it came to style—he could design, or restore, in Tudor, Queen Anne, Georgian, or Arts and Crafts. Roderick Gradidge, himself a passionate but unconventional traditionalist, described him as 'that great Farnham original'.

As he aged, Falkner became more of an oddity, but he never lost his vigour or his clarity of mind. Always too chaotic to maintain his own personal archives, his writing remained sharp and clear. I have quoted him at length, not only to give the flavour of the man but also because his prose is direct and unpretentious.

I have also illustrated the book as far as possible with his own sketches. He may have been a terrible architectural draughtsman, but he could be wonderful as an artist, and he came from the last generation of architects where artistic talent was more highly regarded than structural engineering.

Architects like Falkner could not exist today, but we can still admire his work, and learn from his skills in preserving a townscape, making use of architectural salvage, and showing how an understanding of the past can lead to more interesting architecture in future.

CHAPTER ONE

British Architecture in 1900

In 1900 Harold Falkner was aged 24, very much a child of the late 19th century and just starting on his long 20th-century career as an architect.

The 19th century had been a period of unparalleled prosperity for Britain, generated by massive industrialisation, the development of mines and railways, the climax of British imperial expansion, and a long absence of any major wars. The economic outcome was a burgeoning middle class and an explosion of wealth available for expression in the arts and in building.

Queen Victoria was still on the throne in 1900, but there were new cultural currents stirring. The plays of Oscar Wilde and Bernard Shaw, the rise of socialism, stirred the complacency of the Victorian era. By the time of Victoria's death in 1901 the greater licence of the Edwardian era was a natural development.

All the great scientific developments of the first half of the 20th century which affected building were already available, albeit in their infancy: electricity, concrete, steel, plate-glass, central heating, the telephone and the motor car.

The great cities of Britain had already achieved their pre-eminence, buttressed by huge new suburbs and surrounded by satellite towns from which workers commuted on the new railways. It was now possible to combine the advantages of working in the city with living in the countryside. This was the ambition of the middle classes who were richer than ever, and more numerous too since their numbers were swelled by rentiers, the development of the professions, and by people returning with money and pensions from working overseas. They had come to dominate public life, with strong views on the arts as well as politics.

The Battle of Architectural Styles

Throughout the 19th century there was furious controversy about what the many new public buildings should look like. Up to about 1850 the battle was between the titanic forces of Greek Revival and Gothic Revival, but in later years there were fashions for Italian Renaissance, French Renaissance and what became known as Imperial Baroque, which was thought appropriate for great buildings in London.

There was also a constant questioning, which became even stronger in the 20th century, about whether the Age should develop its own style. In France Viollet-le-Duc wailed, 'Is the 19th century to close without having an architecture of its own?' The architects of the Art Workers' Guild believed passionately in developing a new style, albeit with its roots in the English traditions of the Gothic and Wren, and incorporating elements of the Arts and Crafts movement. There had been great advances in the development of new materials—iron and steel and glass—and their use in buildings, and it was argued that a new 'free style' was more appropriate than mere revivalism.

The battle of the styles was mainly centred around major buildings: churches, town halls, schools, clubs, government offices, and grandiose houses. It became less contentious as it filtered down to more modest domestic buildings, which suddenly provided a bonanza of architectural commissions. It was here that the 'free style' came into its own. The detached suburban house was a special feature of late 19th-century England, whereas its ideal form had previously only been represented by the country parsonage.

From about 1870 until the early 20th century, the years when Falkner was growing up, the favoured style for domestic architecture was 'Queen Anne', though, as stated by its chronicler, Mark Girouard, this had

> comparatively little to do with Queen Anne ... It came with red brick and white-painted sash windows, with curly pediments, steep roofs, and curving bay windows, with wooden balconies and little fancy oriels jutting out where one would least expect them. It was a kind of architectural cocktail, with a little genuine Queen Anne in it, a little Dutch, a little Flemish, a squeeze of Robert Adam, a generous dash of Wren, and a touch of Francois I.[1]

This was the exterior, but the interiors were mainly inspired by the Arts and Crafts Movement.

The Arts and Crafts Movement

The most influential architectural critic in Britain in the 19th century was John Ruskin, a writer rather than an architect. His vast literary output covering the whole field of the arts often carried contradictory messages, but throughout it all runs an admiration for individual craftsmanship, especially medieval craftsmanship.

This taste was taken forward by William Morris (1834-96), friend of the pre-Raphaelites, designer and manufacturer of all types of furnishings, and the main mover in what came to be known as the Arts and Crafts Movement. Painters were initially more influential in this movement than architects, and their work had an obvious impact on stained glass design as exemplified in the work of C.E. Kempe (1837-1907). Both Morris and Kempe initially trained as architects. Morris had worked in the architectural office of G.E. Street, where his colleague was Philip Webb who later designed for him the innovative *Red House* at Bexley in 1859. Morris founded the Arts and Crafts Society and the Society for the Protection of Ancient Buildings, the Kelmscott Press and the leading furnishing firm of the day. His wall-paper designs were, and remain still, enormously fashionable. He provided a salutary example of the way in which architecture could be presented within an overall crafts context.

William Morris represents some of the paradoxes of the Arts and Crafts Movement. As a devotee of simplicity, truth to materials, and unity of design his work can be easily admired, but he sits strangely in an industrial Britain. He lived in a medieval country house at Kelmscott and a Georgian house beside the Thames at Hammersmith. He was implacably opposed to new machinery (including the railways) and mass production. He was a convinced socialist. His work is suffused with nostalgia but he has been viewed by Nikolaus Pevsner and others as one of the pioneers of the Modern Movement in architecture.

As it developed, leading proponents of the Arts and Crafts Movement further debated its paradoxes. Charles Ashbee pondered the problem of whether modern machinery enslaved the true craftsman or whether it helped him by making repetitive work, such as the links in a chain, more easy. Socialists, such as W.R. Lethaby, were concerned that the movement should try harder to design cheap furniture and wallpapers for the masses. The Movement was anti-modern (except in its socialism), anti-industrial and anti-urban, yet its patrons and supporters were people who had made their money in trade and industry, lived in cities, and travelled by rail to enjoy the countryside. They had to be rich enough to pay for individually-made pieces which could never be part of any mass culture.

In 1884 the Art Workers' Guild was founded by a group of young architects from the practice of Norman Shaw—W.R. Lethaby, Ernest Newton, E.S. Prior, Mervyn Macartney. Later William Morris became Master (as in due course did C.F.A. Voysey and Edwin Lutyens), and the architects went beyond the original Gothic ideals to recognise the virtues of Wren and Georgian buildings. In 1888 the Arts & Crafts Exhibition Society was established. In 1896 the Central School of Arts and Crafts was set up in London; its first Director was W. R. Lethaby, an architect who became better known for his Arts and Crafts writings than his buildings.

By the 1890s fashionable taste had shifted slightly towards Art Nouveau, as practised in continental Europe and publicised in England by Aubrey Beardsley, Oscar Wilde and Frank Brangwyn. These men had developed their style from the Arts and Crafts Movement, but were much disliked by the true Arts and Crafts enthusiasts who felt that the sinuous curves lacked the discipline of the Ruskinian Gothic. The only notable British architect who came close to Art Nouveau was Charles Rennie Mackintosh who worked mainly in Scotland. On the whole Art Nouveau was considered unwholesome, representing mere style without any moral content. In the wave of patriotism that swept the country in the Boer War, Art Nouveau was also suspect as being foreign.

In 1891 the movements came together in Compton, near Farnham, to which the great painter and sculptor G.F. Watts moved with his young wife for a new house, *Limnerslease*, designed by Sir Ernest George. Mrs Watts, a supporter of the Home Arts and Industries Association, founded the Compton Pottery works and after her husband's death built the astonishing Memorial Chapel to him in Celtic Revival Style. Another outpost of Arts and Crafts near Farnham was Haslemere Peasant Industries, set up as an artistic community by Godfrey Blount in 1896.

A notable objective of the Arts and Crafts Movement was to get rid of the extraordinary clutter of furnishings and objects which characterised Victorian interiors. The advice of William Morris, as applicable today as a century ago, was 'Have nothing in your house which you do not know to be useful, or believe to be beautiful'.

Despite the death of William Morris in 1896 the Arts and Crafts Movement was still strong in 1900, and kept alive into the early years of the 20th century by young architects such as Edwin Lutyens and M.H. Baillie Scott. It became apparent that it was particularly well suited to small domestic buildings in the country, rather than to big or urban buildings. In the USA it flourished as in Britain, but its influence faded after the 1914-1918 war.

One reason for this was that in England it never overcame the conflict between individual craftsmanship and machine production, which was the only way in which it could be made affordable to more than a privileged few. The London store Liberty's opened in 1875 and by 1900 was marketing mass-produced furniture, ceramics, glass, pewter and cloth in the Arts and Crafts style, but it was disliked by the true Arts and Crafts enthusiasts such as Ashbee, and contributed to the general decline of the Art Workers' Guild after 1900. By contrast, the Deutsche Werkbund, founded in 1907, forged an alliance between craftsmen and manufacturers, such as was later seen in England in the furniture of Heal's.

Falkner's mentor, Reginald Blomfield, led the swing back to the classical style, and successful architects, such as Edwin Lutyens, later followed.

The New Magazines

New ideas in architecture were spread by a flush of new magazines. Improvements in printing techniques, particularly for photographic illustrations, led to the birth of several new illustrated magazines in the late 19th century, mostly designed for the amateur rather than the professional and immensely influential in moulding the tastes and interests of the burgeoning middle classes.

The Studio was founded in 1893 as *An Illustrated Magazine of Fine and Applied Arts*. These included not only pictures and sculpture but also furnishings and architecture, fabrics and wallpapers, and all types of Arts and Crafts.

In 1896 the founders of *The Builders' Journal* started a monthly, *The Architectural Review*, for architects who preferred photographic illustrations to line drawings. Less 'arty' than *The Studio*, it quickly became the preferred journal for professional architects, both modernist and classical, supplanting *The Builder* which had dominated the scene since its foundation in 1842.

In 1897 *Country Life* was founded by Edward Hudson. At first he concentrated on country gentlemen's pursuits such as shooting, hunting and racing, but in 1898 he started the prominent weekly feature on great houses and gardens which became (with increasing scholarship as the 20th century progressed) a prime source for contemporary and historical architectural taste. This was due not only to the scholarship of its writers but also to the skill of its photographers: Charles Latham founded a new school of architectural photography using large plate cameras, bromide prints, and cleverly angled shots. The country house feature appealed greatly to the new rich, and (then as now) generated steady advertising revenue from the estate agents Knight, Frank and Rutley.

Hudson was an early admirer of Lutyens, giving him much publicity and several direct commissions, both in London and in the country. In 1900 he purchased *The Garden* magazine from William Robinson, and subsequently persuaded Gertrude Jekyll, who already wrote for *Country Life,* to become the Editor.

The Taste for the Traditional and Vernacular

The preference of most middle-class clients and their architects was for the traditional and the vernacular. In terms of south-west Surrey this translated into rural rather than urban traditions, for natural materials such as local brick and stone and exposed wooden beams, for roof gables and massive chimneys, for hanging tiles and half-timbering, for carefully carved wood and stone, for heavy oak front doors, for an asymmetric shape, for houses which appeared to have grown organically from their surroundings, for what their advocates believed was simplicity and naturalness. On the negative side it translated into a mistrust of steel and sheet glass, 'progressive' ideas and 'modernism'.

No matter that much of this tradition was invented, much as Scottish traditions were invented in the 19th century, or that it related more to rural life than to the urban housing which was the fate of the majority. It was what the middle classes wanted—and by and large they got it.

For the more conscientious local architects such as Lutyens and Falkner a good source was *Old Cottage and Domestic Architecture in south-west Surrey*, published in 1889 by the architect and antiquary Ralph Nevill. Gertrude Jekyll's book *Old West Surrey* (1904) was based on her pony-trap excursions with the young Lutyens in the early 1890s, when they recorded the houses and artefacts of the area.

The National Trust was founded in 1895. Its membership grew quickly, and further contributed to the traditions, both real and imagined, which are still so popular today.

Indeed, middle-class preferences in the late 19th century were similar to those of the late 20th century when Prince Charles produced his controversial *Vision of Britain*. In vain might architectural progressives inveigh against 'pastiche and sham', 'dishonest architecture', 'synthetic traditions', 'facadism', 'cake designers rather than real architects', 'a futile longing for long lost rural crafts', 'Merrie England' and 'Noddyland', 'farmhouse style transplanted into suburbia'. The most successful architects, such as Norman Shaw who could design to any style, adapted their work to take advantage of their clients' preferences rather than fight them.

For young architects such as Edwin Lutyens there was no doubt about which side they were on, which resulted in their being out of favour with 20th-century modernists and architectural historians of the Pevsner persuasion.

The Architectural Profession in 1900

Since its foundation in 1837, the Royal Institute of British Architects (RIBA) had been the main institution of the profession. But many architects believed passionately that architecture was more of an art than a professional or commercial undertaking, and several resigned when RIBA introduced more stringent professional examinations in 1892. Norman Shaw, arguably the most successful architect of the day, was never a member. He twice refused the prestigious RIBA gold medal, and edited an anthology *Architecture: a Profession or an Art?* which was widely praised.

In the National Census of 1901 there were 10,700 men (no women had yet entered the profession) who called themselves architects, which was one third more than in the Census of 1891. Of these only 1,600 were registered as members of the Royal Institute of British Architects: Falkner himself did not join RIBA until he was over fifty. Part of the reason must have been the dissatisfaction with the idea of examinations and the authority of RIBA, but part also was the fact that then, as now, many people liked to call themselves 'architect' even though they lacked full formal qualifications.

Throughout the 19th century the main path for training architects was the individual private practice, within which older architects could pass on their knowledge, skills and clients to the next generation. Thus Norman Shaw worked under G.E. Street, the great architect of churches and the Law Courts. So did William Morris and Philip Webb. In turn Norman Shaw employed William Lethaby, Ernest George (under whom Lutyens studied) and Ernest Newton. These men dominated Arts and Crafts architecture, though they were also willing to turn their hand to other styles.

The great architectural practices of the day were those of Norman Shaw, Ernest George, Reginald Blomfield, and—less prolific but more prescient—Philip Webb. Each of these trained many pupils in their turn. Already practising in 1900, destined for fame but too young to be truly famous at the time, were C.F.A. Voysey, M.H. Baillie Scott, Hugh Thackeray Turner and Edwin Lutyens (all active in Surrey, though moving onto the national stage), Charles Rennie Mackintosh (in Glasgow), Frank Lloyd Wright (in Chicago), and Herbert Baker (in South Africa).

Outside the office, aspiring architects were encouraged to look, sketch book in hand, at great buildings such as cathedrals, and vernacular buildings such as farmhouses. They were also assigned to work with builders to learn something of their trades. By 1900 domestic houses, rather than churches and great public buildings which had been so important in the 19th century, had become the main business for most architects.

Studying architecture in the 1890s, Falkner was much influenced by these trends. More interested in art than engineering, he was less involved in the way in which architects were experimenting with new materials for big buildings. Iron girders had replaced timber beams. Steel frames had become cheaper and better. Central heating, mostly coal-fired, was common-place. Re-inforced concrete was used in industrial buildings from the 1890s, and in houses from about 1905. As Norman Shaw wrote to W.R. Lethaby in Edwardian times, 'Re-inforced concrete ought to do a lot for us … We have kicked the Gothic Revival out from below our feet, and we are doing "English Renaissance", which we shall kick away too.'

The middle-class English house of 1900

Das englische Haus (first published in 1904 but not available in English translation until 1979[2]) provides a comprehensive and sympathetic description of the English middle-class house of 1900, drawing attention to many aspects which a native English writer might ignore or take for granted. The author Hermann Muthesius, who worked in the German Embassy in London, was an admirer of the English and the English vernacular (including Ruskin-inspired myths about medieval masons), and hated Art Nouveau and 'progressive' architecture. He adored Ruskin, Morris, and the English middle classes, and liked their houses for their 'absolute practicality and unassuming naturalness'.

He praised the leading architects of the day such as Norman Shaw, Ernest George and W.E. Nesfield, but he also recognised the talents of the new generation of C.F.A. Voysey, M.H. Baillie Scott, C.R. Mackintosh ('one of Britain's most outstanding young architects') and Edwin Lutyens (admiring 'his refusal to have anything whatever to do with any new movement').

He particularly liked the tendency of Lutyens and others to relate a house as closely as possible to the surrounding terrain by developing the architectural idea in the form of terraces ('no English house, even a small one, lacks its terrace'), flower beds, pools, box hedges, 'the indispensable lawn', and its architectural appurtenances such as sundials and lead statues, arbours and pergolas, and, less often, gazebos and dovecotes. He noted Lutyens' penchant for loggias with broad semi-circular arches leading onto the garden.

He liked their asymmetrical plans, the exteriors with steeply pitched roofs and overhanging eaves, the interiors with broad upstairs corridors, archways and balconies, and the entrance hall conceived as the key to the plan of the whole house. He noted the strict segregation of the nursery from the rest of the house, the division between residential areas and domestic offices, and the fact that there were rarely communicating doors between the rooms ('the English room is a sort of cage, entered and left by a single door into a corridor, which suits the English desire for seclusion rather than sociability').

He enthusiastically described every aspect of the house and its fittings—the wallpapers, the growing popularity of coloured window glass in halls and at the end of passages, the built-in cupboards ('the most characteristic feature of the modern English bedroom'), the wooden picture rails ('now a permanent feature of every English wall'), and the way the English WC was always a separate room from the bathroom.

He also criticised those aspects he thought to be absurd such as door-knobs ('it is difficult to find any justification for the English habit of using a knob rather than a lever to open a door'), the grand piano in the drawing room ('in view of the fact that the English are probably the most unmusical race in the world the presence of a grand piano in every house is surprising'). He noted that in England the layout of the drawing room was the preserve of the lady of the house, and the necessity for high-backed chairs there since it was always so draughty (he especially disliked the draughts which he saw as being due to the prevalence of sash windows and open fireplaces). He thought it odd that in smaller houses there was no room for the man of the house, albeit that the library and the billiard room fulfilled this role in larger middle-class houses.

He noted that the English house had more servants than a comparable German one as 'the lady of the house merely presides rather than takes part in domestic chores', and the specialisation among servants (generally only maids in the smaller house). Thus the suite of ancillary rooms around the kitchen in which servants performed their specialised functions was twice as many as in a comparable German house ('even the smallest cottage differentiates between the kitchen and the scullery'), and a separate staircase was provided for servants and children.

He devoted many pages to fireplaces, since 'to an Englishman a room without a fireplace is quite unthinkable'. As a German he realised the superior efficiency and economy of the stove and proper draught control (made difficult by sash windows), but he recognised the 'ethical significance' of the fireplace as symbolic of an Englishman's ideas of warm hospitality. Outside, massive chimneys were advertisements for big, hospitable fireplaces. Inside, he noted that the fireplace was often enhanced by inglenooks (especially in dining rooms), architectural chimney-pieces, a full set of fire irons, recesses and panelled walls ('more popular in England than in almost any other country'). Although some houses had central heating by 1900, he noted that even so the fireplace was never omitted from room design.

He praised the widespread use of electric light, which had almost totally replaced gas lighting by 1900, and the way in which Arts and Crafts involvement with metalwork had resulted in light fittings of a high standard (albeit that there was 'a strange adjunct to the light appliance in the form of a material shade'). He also noted the introduction of gas cookers, 'although the kitchen range with its facility for toasting bread and roasting meat and boiling vegetables—English cooking is extremely simple, almost primitive—still dominates'. Though he liked the modernity of English kitchens, and was impressed by the way English children were brought up with good table manners, he contrasted the English dinner party where 'the guests come with no special culinary expectations, with the German style of providing a lavish banquet where the guest is expected to tip the servants'.

He liked and admired the Arts and Crafts Movement even though he realised that the older generation of architects such as Norman Shaw and Ernest George were largely ignorant of it and regarded handicrafts as beneath them. He also saw that Arts and Crafts furniture could never be economically viable on a large scale.

Farnham up to 1900

Throughout his life Falkner was so closely linked with Farnham that any account of his life and work must begin with an account of the town and its surrounding area.

It is an old town. Its origins go back over a thousand years to Saxon times. It straddles the infant River Wey, and the route from London to Winchester via the Hog's Back ridge. Its church and its castle were built by the Normans in the early 12th century. At roughly the same time the Cistercians built their first abbey in

FARNHAM·OLD·TOWN·HALL·1850

1 The old Farnham as pictured by Falkner

England at Waverley, two miles downstream. The medieval pilgrimage route from south-west England to Saint Thomas a Becket's shrine at Canterbury passed through the town.

Farnham's architecture has elements from every century. Its nearby forest and traditional woodworking skills led to Farnham being responsible for the assembly of the great hammerbeam roof of Westminster Hall in 1395. The castle was the home of the Bishops of Winchester (the Church Commissioners own it still) and in 1470 Bishop Wayneflete added a fine brick tower,[3] setting a standard for the quality of brickwork which distinguished Farnham's buildings over the next four hundred years.

It has always been a prosperous place. Domesday Book recorded six water mills. In the 17th century Farnham became the centre of a wheat farming area, and (due to Dutch interference with sea-borne traffic) the conduit through which wheat from West Sussex and south-west England passed to London. Writing in 1673, John Aubrey described Farnham as 'the greatest Market in England for Wheat … sometimes 400 loads are sold in a day'. This was repeated in 1722 by Daniel Defoe: 'Farnham [is], except Hempstead and London, the greatest corn market in England, … a gentleman told me he once counted 1,100 teams of horse, all drawing waggons or carts laden with wheat … But there has been a considerable falling off, on account of the sea carriage to London'. A feature of the town is the number of yards off the main streets where waggons could pull in on market days.

William Cobbett was born in Farnham in 1763, and, after a lifetime writing furious pamphlets about rural England, was buried in the churchyard in 1835. In

2 A Tudor cottage on Firgrove Hill, sketch by Falkner.

the 19th century the surrounding countryside became one of the greatest hop-growing areas. Local businessmen made fortunes trading in hops, and thousands of Londoners arrived every year to help with the hop-picking—and to take a summer holiday.

The prosperity was reflected in its buildings. In Tudor times these were mostly of lathe and plaster, but as the town grew richer these were often replaced—or refaced—with brick. There were many brickworks in the area, but a lack of good local stone apart from the Bargate quarries ten miles away near Godalming.

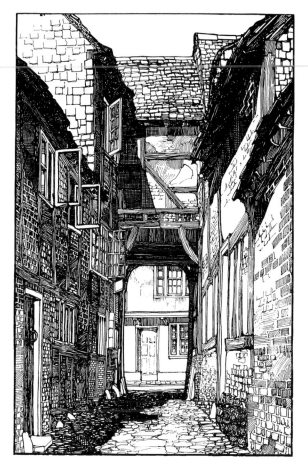 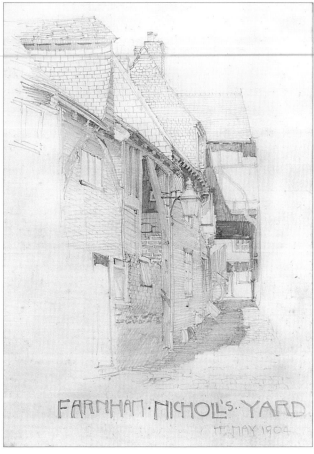

FARNHAM·NICHOLL'S·YARD
H·FALKNER·1904

3 Farnham yards, sketched by Falkner.

Many fine 18th-century houses remained in 1900—and still remain today, thanks to Falkner—especially in Castle Street and West Street, where Falkner lived for most of his life. Willmer House (now the Farnham Museum) in West Street is arguably one of the finest Georgian brick townhouses in the whole of England. Old buildings have survived better in Farnham than many other towns.

Farnham began as an agricultural market town but in the 19th century two developments occurred which brought in money from other sources. In 1849 the railway from London (via Guildford) reached Farnham, making it possible to travel to London in an hour (the railway still operates at the same pace today). This facilitated the development of a commuter population, which grew hugely over the next hundred and fifty years.

Soon afterwards a military town was founded on the heathlands at Aldershot, four miles away. At the time Aldershot had no railway station so the soldiery had to travel to London by train via Farnham station. This was one reason—the hop trade is another—for the extraordinary number of pubs in the town in 1900, especially on the side nearest Aldershot. The soldiery did not live in Farnham, but often their officers chose to do so, and often retired there.

4 Doorways in West Street, Farnham, sketched by Falkner.

Prosperity made Farnham a town where the middle classes predominated. There had never been a great family of landowners, and very few urban proletariat. For many centuries the town was run by the Bishop and his bailiffs. In Falkner's day there was very little industry apart from small-scale brewing, pottery and workshops, with brick and tile making in the surrounding area; most of this disappeared during his lifetime. The great growth of commuters and military and retired people was making Farnham even more predominantly a middle-class town, a trend which accelerated in the 20th century

The implications for architecture, apart from houses of which much more later, were spacious streets and well-tended gardens, a demand for schools, churches, respectable political clubs, some superior shops; and a civic pride concerned with making sure that the town's buildings were deserving of praise.

The area surrounding Farnham, and feeding into it, is fertile farmland. In the 19th century the farmers there were rich and prosperous, as were Falkner's father and grandfather who owned and farmed a substantial area at Dippenhall, on the Hampshire border two miles to the west. The land to the east and south, which is south-west Surrey, is interspersed with areas of heath and pines, less attractive for farming but ideal for people who wanted to have a secluded house in the country that was (after the railway was developed) within easy reach of London. Typical of such families in Falkner's day were the Lutyens and the Jekylls, comfortably middle-class but far from rich.

This was not just an invasion of moneyed Londoners. Among the bankers and businessmen there was a leavening of artists and intellectuals (as indeed both the Lutyens and Jekyll families were). At Compton, a few miles to the east of

5 Willmer House, West Street,
sketch by Falkner.

Farnham, G.F. Watts, the Michelangelo of the day, came to settle with his young
wife. In 1900, a successful playwright even before the launch of *Peter Pan*, J.M.
Barrie came to live at Black Lake Cottage (now called Lobswood Manor) near
Farnham; he ran cricket competitions there and among the participants was
Conan Doyle who lived in Haslemere. There was a sprinkling of intellectual
socialists (Bernard Shaw used to visit Farnham to speak) and a burgeoning Arts
and Crafts Movement which is still strong today.

In 1865 a Farnham School of Art was established. Initially it drew its staff
from the influential South Kensington Art School, among them W.H. Allen who
was so influential in Falkner's career. A close connection between the town and art
teaching has continued to this day, now incorporated in the Surrey Institute of Art
and Design.

There had been a pottery industry in Farnham since Roman times. In 1872
Absalom Harris, whose father married into William Cobbett's family, founded
The Farnham Pottery. He rediscovered the medieval technique of using special clay
dug in Farnham Park to make green-glazed earthenware which had been popular

6 Downing Street, Farnham, sketched by Falkner for his article in *Country Life*.

with Elizabethan lawyers in London. By 1900, with encouragement from W.H. Allen at the Art School, the Pottery was producing much Arts and Crafts ware for sale on a nation-wide basis.

At the end of the 19th century there was still, alongside the incomers, a population of rural craftsmen in the area around Farnham. Their lives were described by George Sturt (1863-1927) in books such as *The Wheelwright's Shop* and *Change in the Village*. He lived in The Bourne, a village being subsumed into South Farnham, and wrote of both the more prosperous craftsmen and the poorer, but fiercely independent, cottagers who tried to make a living from the poorer sandy soil (*Memoirs of a Surrey Labourer*). He viewed such men as the inheritors of a stalwart English tradition, to be cherished in the face of people coming to build new housing in the local villages such as Seale and Elstead and Tilford.

In Falkner's day as now, Farnham stood, socially and geographically, on the cusp between the commuter territory of outer London and the open farmlands of south-west England. The best contemporary accounts of the town architecture are Falkner's own article in *The Architectural Review* of September 1916, and four articles by Christopher Hussey in *Country Life* of July 1942. The centre of the town is still broadly similar today, though the great expansion to the favoured southern area beyond the railway has taken the population from 5,000 in 1900 to over 37,000 a century later.

CHAPTER TWO

Harold Falkner—The Early Years

A Victorian Childhood

The first Falkners came to Dippenhall, just outside Farnham, in 1750. Harold's grandfather farmed there for fifty years and amassed a considerable fortune growing hops. He and his wife died within a month of each other in 1873,[1] and his son, Harold's father Charles, died on 25 June 1875 at the early age of 37. He only wrote his will the day before he died.

Harold Falkner was born on 28 November 1875, five months after the sudden death of his father. It must have been a difficult time for his mother who was aged 39: she had two children already and a third on the way, and her fellow executors believed she should move out of the big family home at Dippenhall House as quickly as possible. A few weeks after her husband's death they moved ten miles away to the White House at Bramley, where Harold was born. The farm stock was sold on 6 October, and the farm was let for 21 years to a Mr Catt with the intention that Charles, the eldest son, should move back there when he became adult (which was exactly what did happen).

The executors in his father's will were his mother Mary, Samuel Arnold, a hop-planter of Runfold House, and Richard Mason, the family solicitor who continued to be involved in Harold's affairs for many years.

There were two older children: a sister named Mary (the same name as her mother) and a brother with the family name of Charles. When they left Dippenhall the intention was that they would move to a smaller house in West Street in Farnham which the family owned, but as it was let out they stayed in Bramley until 1883. From then on, apart from absences in the First World War and when he was living at Stream Cottage, Harold lived in the house at 24 West Street until his death eighty years

7 23/24 West Street—Falkner's house and office for 60 years.

later. It is a late 18th-century brick house, but nothing like as large as many other fine 18th-century brick houses which still stand in West Street. It accommodated the three children, their mother and their aunt, Caroline Watson, and two maids, but there was no proper bathroom and only a small garden.

In his 88th year Harold described his early life in a memoir[2] from which the following quotations are taken. It is evidence both of his sharp memory and of his straightforward style.

'Although my mother was left in what was then known as very comfortable circumstances, her background of parsimonious living had imbued in her a passion for being careful with money. She used to keep private accounts and worry if she was 2d. out. She was able to save about half her income. Among her possessions was the house at 24 West Street, where I now write this.

'My mother's whole life was devoted to her fatherless children, though we children saw little of her unless one of us was ill. We were adequately but not luxuriously catered for. There were three servants—cook, housemaid, and our nurse. The house, to say the least, was chilly. We children slept on the top floor and it was so cold that when we got into bed we kept our feet under us and it was some time before we could lower them to the bottom of the bed. All liquids were frozen by morning and the nurse would bring us hot water in tin cans and we washed in a basin on a washstand that had a cold marble top.

'I remember three rules my mother insisted on being kept—on pain of instant bed or possibly a whacking: never throw food on the fire (there's always the pig bucket); never joke about money; never make remarks about other people's clothing. They are probably wearing the best they can afford.

'Our life before we started school was boring. My only amusements were lead soldiers and (very bad) drawing. My sister was nine years older than me, and therefore no companion; my brother was two years older. My sister had a German governess, who was also allowed to take an interest in Charles and me. I did not like the fraulein: she was a strong advocate of corporal punishment and, having a delicate skin, I was not fond of this.

'But she did enlarge our horizons to some extent. She introduced us to a chemical experiment set from which we learnt some useful things. I remember the fraulein demonstrating the non-conductivity of carbon by holding a kettle of boiling water, cushioned by carbon, in her hand. Unfortunately, though to our great delight, the kettle had been on an open fire and the carbon was glowing and she did get burnt. Our favourite experiment was wrapping iron sulphate slightly moistened in tinfoil and waiting for the explosion.

'I always associated Fraulein Libudch with the German street bands,[3] which, it was understood, brought rain. Anyway, when it rained, these bands often took shelter in Factory Yard, opposite [our house in] 24 West Street, so called because in the 1870's a cloth factory was there. But the days of hand-spinning were over, and the Yard was run down.

'Our windows on the ground floor were protected by wire blinds which more or less kept the dust out. There was perhaps an inch of flint dust on the road surface; it was watered twice a day but if a gig passed midway between waterings it raised a cloud of dust. These blinds, which were topped by a brass rail fastened to the inner sash lining with knobs, allowed people to see out whilst preventing passers-by to see in, though why anyone should have wanted to see in I don't know.

'In wet weather the road was a sea of mud. The process of repairing roads was to scatter about two inches of broken flint and let the wheels of passing vehicles crush it down. The wheels were iron-tyred and the traffic made a big clatter, so that use of bedrooms on the street side of the house was unusual. Nights, too, were noisy; at about midnight the mail coach arrived and unloaded, and at 4 a.m. the brewery men would come clanking up the street, their boots clad with copper for work on the malthouse floor.

'But for all their noise vehicles in the small town of Farnham were few, just the occasional wagon and donkey carts of villagers bringing in vegetables and foodstuffs. I remember a Mrs Gilham bringing us a pair of chicken each week in a well-scrubbed basket with a beautifully laundered napkin. She was the only person we bought from at the door because she was so very clean.

'I joined my brother Charles at the school run by the Misses Alexander at 89 West Street, opposite Vernon House. The young gentlemen were taught by Miss Ellen on the upper floor, and the young ladies by Miss Julia downstairs.'

He goes on to describe his fellow pupils and what happened to them later in life. Some of them achieved national distinction, and all were from local families. Among them were the young Knights from Knights Bank, owners of a notable building which Falkner later demolished.

'Their sister was my first love; she was seven and I was six. All I can remember is that she married and had children; also that she was awarded a Royal Humane Society medal.

'Charles left for boarding school and later I went too. My new school was a filthy hole, run by a clergyman who took a few select boys to educate with his sons. I was the youngest boy. There were not enough of us to form a football team and on Saturdays we were left to our own devices. We generally walked to Guildford and back; the fare was 3 pence and, as this was one of my mother's economies, this was all I got for pocket-money.

'I will say this for the school: we were quite well fed. Meat was plentiful and relatively cheap in those days. I can remember huge joints of meat from which the cuts were liberal. I learnt nothing there. … I eventually decided life was far more pleasant at home and resolved to do something about it. The station being handy, one day I jumped the gates just as the train was coming in and I was free. I threatened suicide if I was sent back. It was the best single action I had ever taken. The school was broken up two years later and my brother went to Churchers College, Petersfield, where he learnt to play cricket but very little else.'

Falkner then expands at length on their diet: the breakfasts of cold ham, the big joints of beef for Sunday dinner, the favourite suet pudding. Water being suspect, the adults drank beer (grandfather even had it with breakfast) purchased from the *Lion and Lamb* and kept in a barrel in the cellar, and the children were given various nauseous cordials. Food seemed much more important in the house than warmth, either physical or maternal.

'On the whole, life was dull. We played few games. We were not allowed to mix with common little boys. Occasionally we visited family friends. At children's parties we played Musical Chairs, Hunt the Slipper and other stupid parlour games. In one game of Charades at the Masons, I was the long lost boy who came down the chimney to be embraced by his mother. Addy Mason, acting the role of mother, was the centre of a slight rumpus because I had overdone the soot part.

'In retrospect I can see that the Victorian way of life was drab, despite the nostalgic yearnings of certain modern writers who have not experienced it. One thinks immediately of the absurd clothes that women wore when they became slaves to fashion magazines which promoted the designs of London and Paris dressmakers. The middle-class women could afford the whims of fashion, giving away last year's models to poorer women, often with ludicrous results.

'Victorian furniture, too, was ugly … heavily curved and carved. The four-poster bed's successor gave way to iron bedsteads with brass knobs. The Victorians desecrated their homes too. Old panelling was torn from the walls and paper substituted. Georgian wooden mantelpieces were replaced with marble ones of atrocious design, later considered cold and covered with mantel boards having a cloth border, and curtains trimmed with chenille balls. Building design suffered: speculative builders put up red brick villas with white dressings and slate roofs—never mind, they would fall down in forty years, but, alas, they are still with us. The rage was all for great slabs of plate glass in windows; most of Bath was degraded by having sash bars torn out and single sheets inserted.

'Life was very dull in Victorian times. One meliorating feature was being taken for a walk by our nurse on fine days. Outside the town, Farnham was one vast hopfield; the bines provided a pleasant shade on a hot day. One could walk to Dippenhall three different ways and have hops on each side. The roadways were unpleasant, for they had a surface of chalky dust, which was stirred whenever a gig went by. South of the river were the Bishops Meadows and one could walk along the river bank from Weydon Mill to the Hatches. The river was always fuller when banked up for the mill.

'On our longer walks the attraction used to be Mrs Robinson's in East Street, the only shop in the town exclusively selling sweets. In the stretch of river between the Guildford Road junction and Bourne Mill, men and boys could be seen bathing. The mill was always a delight; the wing had not yet been cut off [for road-widening] and formed a secluded forecourt. Sometimes there was a peacock there—my most treasured childhood memory. And the mill wheel, which gave a great display right on the road, and, up the little hill on the west, the waterfall, a constant source of delight, terrific in flood but just a trickle in times of drought.

'Up the Tilford Road. too, it was all hops. Just over the top of the hill, a footpath ran between hedges and a little further down the hill there was another path which led through woodlands to Waverley [Abbey].

'When the time came to take education seriously—and indeed I was eager to start learning—Charles Stroud of the Farnham Grammar School was engaged to come in for an hour each evening to cram me, principally in maths and literature. I must have done fairly well for we got through the first book of Euclid in no time and even went on to solids. Then one day I was invited to the annual breaking-up party at his school next door. It was a great success and I thought that if a master could take all this trouble to entertain us then it must be a pretty good school. So I decided to go there. The Farnham Grammar School then had a rough reputation, but as it was next door to where I lived, I could easily escape.

'Mostly the boys were the sons of local tradesmen. Many were in poor circumstances for it was a time of recession in Farnham's mainstay, the hop industry. The final coup had been administered by the new Tithe Appropriation Act, one of Gladstone's worst offences. I can remember counting as many as thirty empty properties in the town, thirteen of them being shops in The Borough. Bankruptcies were frequent …

'I have a photograph of the Grammar School at that time. Most of the boys are in clothes obviously cut down and adapted. I was put into the fourth form and was soon at the top of it. A.J. Stevens and Cyril Garbett (later Archbishop of York) were in the third form; they used to come to school on ponies and wore corduroy trousers which on wet days gave off an affluvia [*sic*] hence their sobriquet "Little Stinker".

'Justice was rough. A boy found guilty of sneaking or other unsocial crimes was laid across parallel bars in the playground and beaten with a cricket stump. I only incurred this punishment once; I was proud of my knowledge of Euclid and one day in class I recited ad lib the pons asinorem theorem. Found guilty of showing off, I received three strokes of the stump.

'Charles Stroud had been head boy at a school in Winchester where, I fancy, the regime had been medieval. We had a peculiar system of education. The School was desperately poor, being an old foundation depending on a grant of land which was very nearly tenantless or let at very low rents, and governed by persons appointed by the Vestry whose sole function was to present the prizes. Emphasis was on the sciences, with a different subject each term—Geology; Agriculture; Electricity and Magnetism; Sound, Light and Heat; Hygiene and Physiology. These in the early stages were easy enough.

'Finally I got into the Lower Fifth and this was not so easy. In the Upper Fifth it was the thing not to do one's homework and naturally I followed this practice. And so I drifted to the top of the school, my only rival being Isidore Phillips, who lost marks on Drawing and Religious Instruction. I introduced playground football, but the balls wore out quickly on the gravel surface. The only soccer we had was in the Park, by the dell in front of the Keeper's House; this was after school and on Wednesday and Saturday half-holidays—we needed more practice.'

Harold loved sports—not only football but also swimming and cricket. At Farnham Grammar School, 1886-91, he also won many academic prizes. He seems to have been a popular boy, which was important later in life since the Grammar School old boys tended to dominate local business and politics. Among his contemporaries at school were Charles Borelli and Walter Elphick, both later prominent citizens.

'I left the Grammar School at the age of sixteen. I had already been to evening classes at the School of Art and now I became an all-day student. I was provided with monumental tomes on Classic Architecture written by a German. Nothing could have been more discouraging, but fortunately I had the constant attention of W.H. Allen, who knew a lot about architecture from the Italian aspect.'

This was a crucial turning point in Falkner's life. A talented teacher converted a teenage boy, who one might expect to be self-absorbed, rebellious, and interested only in physical pursuits, to a lifelong interest in the arts. Under the influence of Allen he abandoned his childhood ambition to become a vet. Veterinary work might have fitted better with his family's farming background but he related later in life that he had also been influenced by noticing that in one house a visiting architect was offered a glass of sherry while the visiting vet was sent below stairs for his hospitality.

Allen[4] had trained at the Royal College of Art in South Kensington which was at the time the leading art college in England, promulgating the principles of William Morris and the connection between arts and crafts. Among others, Gertrude Jekyll was a student there earlier, and Edwin Lutyens rather later. Allen

8 Harold Falkner as a young teenager.

remained at Farnham Art School until 1928, influencing two generations, painting many water-colours (later bequeathed to museums at Alton and Farnham), and taking a lively interest in all aspects of local arts and crafts.

Recalling this time many years later Harold wrote:[5]

'Allen transformed our outlook, which thought nothing of our Georgian past and relegated its furniture to the attics if it was not sawn up. Allen furnished his house with local Chippendale and Sheraton, opening our eyes to a new world. I began to realise there was a good deal in the craftsmanship and general design of Georgian buildings which suited it to the requirements of the modern householder: its thick walls, its tiled roof, the relationship of its windows and wall spaces. In fact we began to realise that we were the caretakers of buildings that ought, and were just beginning, to be appreciated.'

Throughout his life Falkner repeated his assertion that 'Farnham owes to Allen everything that is of value.' In particular he learned from Allen two skills which he loved and continued to practise with great skill throughout his life: sketching and wood-carving.

Training to be an Architect

Having decided to become an architect, he followed his guardian's advice to work as a builder's apprentice. He was attached for two years to a local building firm, Tompsett and Kingham, successors to Frank Birch of Longbridge, Farnham. Falkner wrote in his memoir: 'I knew John Kingham personally as a joint member of the Tennis Club. He was rather a superior type of builder. His father had invested £10,000 in the business when John took over from Frank Birch.' He recalled that he did not learn as much as he might. He much preferred the joiner's shop to the office, and spent many happy hours learning to carve mouldings.

> 'If I had been more industrious, and if I had not been treated so much as a parlour-boarder, I might have learned quite a lot; as it was, I did discover that a panelled door is not hewn out of one piece, and I saw quite a lot of the relations between builder and architect. But above all, the builder had done nearly all Norman Shaw's early country work, and had a storehouse of drawings, details, and all the notes. We also did a job for Voysey, [and] very nearly, but not quite, one for Lutyens.[6]

The Birch[7] family had been involved in building in Farnham since the early 19th Century. Frank Birch was one of Norman Shaw's favourite builders: they had worked together on Knight's Bank in Farnham in 1867, and on *Pierrepont*, the mansion at Millbridge near Farnham, in 1876. The job for Voysey was *Lowicks* at Frensham in 1894, about the time Falkner left his apprenticeship (Voysey's other country houses near Farnham, *Greyfriars* at Puttenham in 1896 and *Norney* at Shackleford in 1897, came later). Both Norman Shaw and Voysey were important influences on Falkner's architecture.

The job for Lutyens was probably *Crooksbury House*, Lutyens' first major commission: although Birch did not get this job he worked on another nearby, which enabled Falkner to scrutinise Lutyens' work. He became an admirer of Lutyens, but wrote perceptively that *Crooksbury* as it was built initially 'was nothing to write home about'. He was much more complimentary about Lutyens' later extensions to the house, which he felt incorporated everything that was best about English architecture.

After two years as a builder's apprentice, Falkner was ready to move on to the next stage of his architectural training. This was, he wrote later:[8]

> 'before the days of architectural schools, and the recognised way of getting into the profession was to go as a pupil, generally for three years, to a practising architect. On the whole it worked well. The successful man could run his office on his pupils' premiums and work, and the pupils saw the way the business was conducted, and could, if they so chose, learn a good deal. But it was not to be supposed that the principal would waste his time on them; in fact cases were known in which the great man did not know some of his pupils by sight.'

In this context it was perhaps as well that Harold did not get the place he wanted in the office of Norman Shaw, the most famous architect of the day but already aged 60 and with over eighty[9] would-be pupils on his waiting list; a few years earlier Lutyens had been similarly disappointed. Many years later Harold recalled that 'Shaw having no vacancies it was a toss up whether I should be articled to Lutyens or Blomfield and by mere laziness I chose [the office of Reginald] Blomfield.' In fact it is unlikely that there would have been a vacancy with Lutyens, who only set up a proper London office in 1898.

'Blomfield in those days was the coming young man—red-headed and bearded, something between the portraits of Drake and the Wills' tobacco advertisement, full of energy, with a perfect Oxford manner, and a background of a double first, MA Oxon. He had established himself at 1, New Court, Temple. Approached by Middle Temple lane, across Fountain Court, it is (or was) one of the most beautiful early Georgian buildings in London, possibly designed by Wren himself. It certainly had a very fine effect on the clients, and I believe RTB[lomfield] lived on the third floor so that the effect of the AD 1700 staircase and the names of our eminent co-tenants could soak in.'

9 Sir Reginald Blomfield drawn by Ginsbury, *c.*1906.

Falkner recalled that Blomfield was doing some good work at the time, though it began to fall off and pupils were reduced to inking in old drawings. In fact, Blomfield's fame and principal work as an architect came after 1900, with a knighthood and presidency of RIBA at the end of the Edwardian period. When Falkner worked for him he had more of a reputation as an author. In 1892 he had published *The Formal Garden in England* which stirred up a bitter controversy (described in Chapter 5) with the leading gardening writer of the day, William Robinson. When Falkner was his pupil he was working on his major work, published in 1897, *A History of Renaissance Architecture in England 1500-1800.*

Blomfield was an honorary secretary of the Art Workers' Guild in 1892, but resigned in 1895 as he attended meetings so infrequently; he was also a partner in a furniture firm founded by architects with Arts and Crafts sympathies. In fact he became increasingly more sympathetic to the work of Wren and the Georgians rather than the Arts and Crafts Movement. His influence may explain why Falkner began his career with a sort of 'Wrenaissance' style, and only later in life moved to a fascination with the English vernacular of barns and farmhouses.

Falkner commuted by train from Farnham to London, which he described many years later:

'I remember the getting up, and the hurried breakfast, and the rush to the train. The train journey much as it is today (things don't change much on the

Southern [Railway] in forty years) and the walk across Waterloo Bridge which always seemed to be hot and dusty.

'As one crossed Waterloo Bridge on a sunny day, looking towards Somerset House on the right, with all the City spires (there were no concrete blocks to hide them then) and St Paul's in the distance, the view was an education in itself. And then into the coolness of the Strand with all its early morning smells—the grocer, of bacon, cheese and sawdust; the florist, of stephanotis, tuberose and wallflower; the restaurants of soup, and the pubs of beer. It was quite another story in the late afternoon when the sun got round; the smells got stale and mingled with asphalt and horse manure.

'And so through Wren's Middle Temple gate and down Temple Lane, and across Fountain Court, nearly the finest architectural setting in Europe, in May with its early-leafed lime trees shade, into New Court, Temple, meeting perhaps the charwoman and her brushes departing round the corner, and Sir Richard's man taking his wig to be refurbished before the courts opened. Up the wide shallow stairs (said to have been detailed by Wren himself) past the half-opened door of Lord James' outer office, with its dusty smell and calf-bound books to the ceiling, the office of two Lords of Appeal, and on the top floor Sir (Mr then) Reginald Blomfield's office. He asked us how we looked—well, we should look a bit strange today.

'Morning coats and pin-striped trousers were essential; top-hats not discouraged; that's the way I began, but I developed into a hat and coat something like Sandeman's port-wine poster before I left.

'We were never very busy except once when we had a competition. My idea of inking in a drawing and Sir Reginald's did not coincide, so I was not overworked. And of our attitude towards the gods, the god of gods was [Norman] Shaw. If there was a good job going Shaw got it. If he didn't want it anyone might have it. ... Shaw was particularly acceptable to us, the 'immature classicists', Jackson, Belcher, Bryden and Blomfield, in that he was turning from Romantic Gothic to Classic.'

Falkner was not sentimental about the past:

'Although there was no petrol [pollution] horse traffic produced manure, which in wet weather became stinking mud, in dry a dangerous dust. The office was often too cold, and at other times much too hot. The lot of the well-to-do was tolerable but of the poor damnably bad. Children in rags, obviously inadequately fed, were sent to beg in the streets ... I always remember them on Hungerford Bridge (out of sight of the police) ... They used at least to make me feel uncomfortable. We were told that if we gave them pennies their mothers would only spend them on gin, and at weekends I was usually broke.

'Our political outlook was strongly Leftish, the sort of not very practical Socialism which Ruskin, Morris and Walter Crane preached—a comfortable sort of creed which promised a three-course (at least) dinner and a sound bottle of wine for everyone.'

In architecture:

'We hoped to pick up the threads of the Georgian tradition where it had gone to bits in the 1830-1850's. I myself was a little torn between the architecture of Philip Webb (Morris' influence) which relied on craftsmanship and material—what Rickards called "rabbit-hutch stuff"—and the Georgian tradition. I had had a good deal of experience as a carver, and the "rabbit-hutch stuff" was more interesting than doing a yard or two of the same pattern on a Classic moulding. It was a combination of these two themes that partially accounted for Lutyens' subsequent triumph.

'The Art Workers' Guild was a movement of great promise. Craftsmen, architects (select), painters and sculptors met at Clifford's Inn hall once a month. Someone read a paper, there were drinks, by no means teetotal, and a discussion, sometimes hilarious, often furious. There was even a junior branch, to which I, as RB's pupil, was admitted. ... [At the] Easter revels the crowning effort was the Masque at the Guildhall, in which both branches performed. Lethaby designed the properties, and, I think, everyone their own dresses. I remember Mrs Ashbee loaded with practically the whole stock-in-trade—her husband was a jeweller.

'The world between 1875-1895 was an ugly place so far as its current production of architecture was concerned. the number of architects in England who were producing even tolerable stuff could be counted on the fingers; the rest were really terrible. ... The Victoria and Albert Museum and the Imperial Institute are typical examples of the period. "Originality", as it was called, was at a premium, and it really amounted to little more than jumbling up half a dozen styles and adding a little personal vulgarity.

'Not only the buildings but the furniture, textiles, crockery, glass, silver, and everything that could be made and sold was bad. The machine had taken the bit between its teeth and run away with itself. Also it had so cheapened things that there was an enormous surplus. The typical drawing room of the time was cluttered to an unbelievable extent with nicknacks, whatnots, plush-framed photographs, chenille-balled mantelboards and polar-bear hearthrugs so that movement was positively dangerous. In order to dispose of their rubbish manufacturers had constantly to change the fashion, so that last year's things could be discarded in favour of the even more awful creations of this. ... This was the sort of thing the Art Workers' Guild set out to reform ... they eschewed commercialism ... but without some sort of commercialism there can be no expansion, and the effect was, I fear, only to add a little tolerably good stuff to the original pile of rubbish.

'This craze for change of "fashion" had another very dangerous contingency. The perpetrators of these horrors were very well satisfied with their efforts, and were a constant danger to anything old, or, as they would say, out of date; consequently, old furniture, old buildings, or anything decent, were in constant danger. To counter this (and the craze for restoration) Morris had founded the Society for the Preservation of Ancient Buildings.

Falkner was sceptical about what seemed to him to be another destructive agent, the concern with sanitation which led to so many old buildings being 'sacrificed'.

> 'Sanitary appliances were in a rudimentary state, and were more useful in conveying gases and germs from the sewers to the houses than from the houses to the sewers, and, as the older the houses generally the older the drains, every old house was, in the eyes of the Ministry of Health and the sanitary inspector, a potential death-trap.'

He was more enthusiastic about

> 'the visits, which were encouraged, to specialist manufacturers who particularly catered for the [architectural] profession … the makers of ironwork, door-furniture and lead-work, almost exclusively to the designs of the elect … the plasterers with a continuity right back to Georgian times … the Dutch tiler whose Persian tiles I still want to buy … Lowndes and Drury, the great glass-workers; Aumonier, the carver, of whom I was always afraid—he knew so much.'

As a junior member of the Art Workers' Guild, he came to know many of the influential architects of his generation, such as A.J. Penty, Cecil Brewer, W. Curtis Green, and Ambrose Heal who opened a furniture shop in Tottenham Court Road which set (and still maintains) the style for quality furniture.

One gets an impression of a sensitive, fun-loving young man, keen on swimming and sport and speed in general. His smart appearance is confirmed by a picture at the wedding of his sister in October 1887 to R.W. Mason: Harold was an usher and two of the bridesmaids were his cousins on his mother's side, Mary and Dorothy Attlee (also related to Britain's Prime Minister of 1945-50). His brother-in-law taught him to swim, and he often spent his summer holidays at Eastbourne. Unusually for an aspiring architect, he never went to continental Europe.

First Years as an Architect

When he reached the age of 21, in November 1896, he inherited £10,000 (including houses at 24 West Street, Bourne Farm and Firgrove Hill) under the terms of his father's will. A sum of this size, nearer £1 million in today's money, might seem what any young man most needed. But in the view of his subsequent partner, Guy Maxwell Aylwin, it spoilt his architectural career by removing the need to strive for business and to be meticulous in devoting time to the less interesting aspects such as building regulations.

He decided to leave Blomfield and set up on his own in Farnham, without bothering to sit the exams to become an Associate of the Royal Institute of British Architects (RIBA). He did not join RIBA until 1927, when Aylwin proposed him as a Fellow.

One of his first projects was a bathroom extension for the family home in West Street. His mother was delighted with it—very few houses in Farnham at the time had the luxury of a bathroom—but she died shortly afterwards in January 1897. Thereafter the house was wholly his own: both his brother and his sister had moved away on marriage, though his aunt Caroline Watson ran it for him until her death in 1926. Throughout his life it was also his office.

Thus by age 21 he had inherited both a fortune and a house and office. What a contrast to his contemporary, Edwin Lutyens, also brought up near Farnham but with very little basic education and surrounded by 13 brothers and sisters. Six years older than Falkner, he had started his business as an architect at age 20 without sitting the RIBA exams but a £100 legacy and a single commission obtained through a family friend.

A key family friend in Harold's early life was Richard Mason, a local solicitor who was one of his father's trustees (and thus Harold's guardian) and who also married Harold's older sister Mary. Mason was much involved in Farnham town matters and later became Town Clerk (where he did not always see eye to eye with HF). In 1897 he was Secretary of a committee formed to commemorate Queen Victoria's Diamond Jubilee.

10 The 'key that fortunately turned in the lock' (as illustrated in *The Artist*, 1901).

One of their projects was to build a swimming bath to replace the bathing in the river enjoyed by boys and young men. 'Bathing drawers were almost unknown and in any case would have been despised by bathers in the river, which fact was very attractive to nursemaids and others in the Guildford Road a hundred yards away. But this did not suit the non-conformist conscience.[11]' At his brother-in-law's request Harold made up the £100 shortfall between the donations and cost, and agreed to act as honorary architect. The site was next to the new Farnham Liberal Club, an early (1895) building by Edwin Lutyens in the Queen Anne style.

This was Harold's first outside commission, albeit that he earned no fee. It was completed at a cost of £800, and officially opened by the Duchess of Albany for whom Harold had designed (and Borelli cast) a special gilt key 'which fortunately turned in the lock.' It was a constant financial struggle to keep the Bath open. In the 1920s it was handed over to the Urban District Council and an extra pool added. It was

11 Strangers Corner—Falkner's sketch of the studio addition.

closed in the 1980s when a new Sports Centre was built, and later reborn as a public garden under the auspices of the Farnham Swimming Baths Trust. It still has problems with usage and finance, but there remains the fronting brick arch with Arts and Crafts lettering personally carved by Harold himself. When asked why his lettering referred to the Queen as Victoria I, he replied that there might be other Queen Victorias later—and indeed Elizabeth II might have been a Victoria II.

His second commission was to design a house, Strangers Corner, for his old art master W.H. Allen. This house, still outwardly very much as he left it and clearly visible from the road, is a truly remarkable achievement, a fine example of the fashionable 'Wrenaissance' style (see Fig. 11 and Plate I), built in 1897. He was called back later to add a studio wing (illustrated in *The Builders Journal* 6 August 1902). This has a rendered exterior, which contrasts with the bare brick of the main building. The studio itself is upstairs, a panelled room with stained wooden beams (apparently serving no structural purpose) and lit with a tall mullioned window with a curved top. It says much for Allen's perception that he should have entrusted the design to a 21-year-old, but he was certainly delighted with it, painted several pictures of it, and lived there happily until 1932.

Before Falkner set up in business there was not a lot of competition among Farnham architects. He recalled[12] that

'In Farnham in the eighties there were two oldish men practising—Mr Wonnacott, a prominent Free Church man who would not build a pub; the other Mr Stapley who had no such prejudices. … Then, about 1890 a young 'architect by profession' arrived on the scene. The Institute in South Street was built and is typical; we have progressed. Tiles take the place of slates, red brick supersedes yellow, there is a wealth of ornament, windows have bars in the upper but not in the lower sashes; it is probably inspired by Norman Shaw, with such modifications as might be expected to appeal to the rustic mind. There is no sign of appreciation of eighteenth century work. In fact, when a Georgian building had to be replaced, as in the case of the old Grammar School, it was done in a modified Gothic.'

The young Lutyens might have been a competitor, having grown up in Thursley near Farnham and obtained all his early work in the neighbourhood. He was only six years older than Falkner but by 1897 he was married and had moved his office to London.

In 1900 a London architect, David Niven (1864-1942), came to live in Farnham. In partnership with Herbert Wigglesworth he had designed interiors for Castle Line ships and built some houses in the commuter areas around London. They had an art nouveau style and were keen to expand their business in Surrey. At Niven's suggestion Harold Falkner joined them in 1900, and the firm was thereafter known as Niven, Wigglesworth and Falkner. Harold did not always get on well with his partners, despite their much greater experience, and left the partnership in 1903 (though the partnership name survived until 1909). It is not possible to say which of the houses they designed is exclusively Falkner's work, but there is a general presumption (substantiated by his initials on published sketches) that any NWF buildings in the Farnham area in the period 1900-06 were principally Harold Falkner.

A subsequent pupil of Niven and Wigglesworth was Guy Maxwell Aylwin (1889-1968) who also lived in West Street, Farnham, and formed a partnership with Falkner in 1927-30 (see Chapter 6).

Harold Falkner as a Young Man

His niece, Beryl Falkner, described him in an interview for *The Farnham Herald* on 29 August 1980. She knew him well when she was growing up as the daughter of his elder brother Charles at Dippenhall House, and had fond memories of his visits there, remembering him as

> a fun-loving young man in Edwardian Farnham who liked to play with her own and her brother's toys when he visited Dippenhall House, and who brought them big boxes of candied fruits at Christmas. He loved dogs … [he was] a man who relished good conversation and good food (especially chocolate eclairs), who enjoyed a game of golf [he was a member of the Club at The Sands] or chess and liked the theatre both in London and in Farnham. An impatient man, the challenge of speed appealed to him—skating and cycling as a boy, motor cycles and cars in their early days, the first planes.[13]

As a young man he continued to sketch, both in Farnham and in other English towns. His pencil drawings, some of which were published in the architectural press and others now in the Farnham Museum, show great talent (as described later in Chapter 8). In 1900 his drawings were shown at the Royal Academy and in *The Architectural Review*. This was the start of half a century of having his articles, sketches and letters published in the national architectural press.

When the First World War broke out he was nearly forty, but volunteered immediately. He was posted to the Royal Engineers as a despatch rider (a job that would have appealed to his love of speed, but took no account of his age or architectural qualifications). A year later, when he was stationed as a Corporal at Carlow in Ireland (the only time he ever left England—which was unusual for an artist-architect) he injured his leg in a motor cycle accident, almost died when septicaemia set in at the military hospital in Aldershot, and was left with a limp for the rest of his life. After recovering he again enlisted and in April 1918, to his delight, was gazetted a Second Lieutenant in the Royal Flying Corps. After the war was over he returned to 24 West Street in Farnham where his Aunt Caroline, assisted by two maids, continued to keep house for him until her death in 1926. His business continued to flourish, but he was less of the smart young man and more of the eccentric figure of later years.

Why did he never marry? With three women (an aunt and two maids) to look after him and a comfortable home of his own he did not have the usual pressures. Perhaps he wanted to remain a free agent. Perhaps, like many other people, he was just not 'the marrying kind'. Some might seek a more specific explanation. A century ago one might have explained it by an unhappy love affair (of which there have been rumours) or unrequited love, but this assumes that it is impossible to fall in love a second time. Today one might explain it by hints of homosexuality or lack of a sex drive, but there is not the slightest evidence of this. It also assumes that the initiative in getting married lies wholly with the man, and never with the woman. Even if Harold took no initiative himself surely there would have been women who might have chased him?

As a young man he was handsome, even dashing, with a lively sense of humour and a love of children and animals. Tall and full of energy, he enjoyed sport, the theatre and fast cars. He dressed elegantly. He came from a prominent local family; he owned a substantial house, had a fortune in the bank, and a respected professional business. He reached the age of 40 as a single man when there was suddenly, due to World War I, a dearth of eligible single men.

A lady who knew Harold when he was old and she was a girl is Sylvia Morgan, daughter of Frank Morgan, headmaster of Farnham Grammar School and a close friend of Harold. He came round regularly to listen to classical music at their house. She and her mother thought him a charming man beneath his brusque exterior, which her mother ascribed to his motor accident. 'We knew him as a cultivated man, a good conversationalist, with a keen sense of humour and brilliant blue eyes—he must have been very handsome as a young man. He was certainly interested in women—I remember him describing one as having the prettiest knees in Farnham.' Perhaps if he had married he might never have become the brusque eccentric whom old people in Farnham remembered at the end of the 20th century.

Falkner and Lutyens

There are many similarities between the early lives of Falkner and Lutyens, and it would not have been unreasonable, if one compared them both in their early 20s, to expect Falkner to have the more successful career.

They were born within a few miles of each other in south-west Surrey, and a few years of each other (Lutyens being six years older). Falkner had a better education at Farnham Grammar School, while Lutyens spent only a short time in formal education and learned more from hanging around the local carpenter in

Thursley. Falkner learned as much about art under W.H. Allen as Lutyens did in South Kensington, and his early sketches showed more promise than anything drawn by Lutyens.

Falkner did a proper apprenticeship with a more reputable building firm than Lutyens'. For both young men Norman Shaw's office was the first choice for their architectural pupil-ship; both were put off by the long waiting list, and made do with another leading London architect of the day; again, Falkner's choice of Blomfield was arguably more promising.

Both young men left their architectural mentor without taking their RIBA exams, and both set up their own architectural practice in their early 20s. But Falkner had a proper office in a house that he owned, and came from a family which was widely respected in the area. He also linked up with two more experienced architects to widen his expertise and his contacts. Both young men were befriended early in their early 20's by Gertrude Jekyll, as described in Chapter 5, and knew each other through their friendship with her. From such similar beginnings Lutyens' career took off spectacularly—but Falkner's did not. Why?

Was it because Lutyens was more ambitious, both for fame and to escape his father's penury? Was it because, in pursuit of his ambitions, Lutyens married the daughter of an earl—while Falkner never married? Once launched in a higher social stratum, Lutyens made the most of country house parties to seek potential clients.

Was it because, as his one-time partner G.M. Aylwin suggested, Falkner's inheritance of plenty of money at age 21 meant that he never had to try harder, to win clients or even to comply with boring building regulations?

Coincidentally, another local architect, W. Curtis Green who was born in Alton near Farnham, was invited to run Lutyens' office while he was away in India. Curtis Green was an exact contemporary of Falkner and a fellow member of the Junior Art Workers' Guild, very much an artist-architect who loved rural vernacular styles. His *Old Cottages and Farmhouses of Surrey* (1908), illustrated with many of his sketches, covered similar ground to Ralph Nevill, whose book had so interested Lutyens and Falkner. Yet he went on to design many prominent buildings in London, including the Dorchester Hotel where he was called in to make the starkly modernist exterior more attractive. His career demonstrates that it was possible for a traditionalist architect to move to London and survive successfully under the Modern Movement. Why did Falkner never take this route?

The complimentary article about him in the September 1901 issue of *The Artist* said that 'his health forbids his dwelling in town … and with such a charming old house as he owns [in Farnham] who would desire that he come to the hum and roar of the metropolis.' The suggestion of ill-health was nonsense in a young man who played a variety of sports, but the comfortable nature of his life and friendships in Farnham would not have spurred someone lacking a strong sense of personal ambition.

CHAPTER THREE

Farnham—The Garden Suburb

The Garden Suburb Movement

Falkner began his career as an architect at a time when the concept of the Garden Suburb was being developed all over England. It accounted for by far the largest part of the new building in Farnham in the early 20th century, and provided the bulk of his business for the first 30 years of his practice.

In the early 19th century John Nash had introduced the idea of building instant villages in picturesque style, at Blaise Hamlet near Bristol and [Regent's] Park Villages in London; albeit that they were just middle-class housing estates they attracted widespread praise. In the middle of the 19th century some industrialists built model villages in rural surroundings for their workers—Saltaire, Port Sunlight, Bournville.

Towards the end of the 19th century the idea of a planned garden city had begun to take hold on people's imagination. The key idea was that, in an industrial age, people should live in planned communities surrounded by space and greenery: not only would this be conducive to good health, it was also thought that it might make for happier lives and a better adjusted society in general. In 1898 Ebenezer Howard published his seminal book on Garden Cities, and his ideas were put into practice at Letchworth from 1903 and subsequently in Welwyn Garden City. The first Directors of Letchworth included Joseph Rowntree, Edward Cadbury and W.H. Lever, all of whom, apart from being important in obtaining financial backing, were also involved in garden villages for their own workers.

The Garden Suburb was an offshoot of these ideas. Facilitated by the spread of new railway lines, including the underground railways in London, middle-class people were able to live further from their work and enjoy the promise of domestic space. Although the countryside was acknowledged to be the best environment it was not possible for the majority to live there but the suburb was a reasonable compromise if it could be made to look like the countryside.

The illusion was fostered by gardens, trees, hedges, and lawns. Streets were laid out to be curving rather than in a grid plan, there were bye-laws concerning road widths and drainage, churches and (in some cases) shops and pubs, but nothing was to be higher than four floors and basements disappeared on grounds of health.

To be fully effective a garden suburb required an overall developer. The first proper garden suburb was Bedford Park, developed on 113 acres in West London by Jonathan Carr in 1875. Many of the houses were designed by Norman Shaw, often in a vaguely Queen Anne style, and the village atmosphere was fostered by wooden (rather than iron) balconies and lots of trees. It quickly became popular with middle-class people of progressive tastes, the sort of people who loved the drawings of Kate Greenaway and Randolph Caldecott.

The next great development of this type was Letchworth Garden City, designed by Raymond Unwin who had sat at the feet of Ruskin and imbibed socialism from William Morris. He went on to become overall architect and planner for Hampstead Garden Suburb, started in 1906 by Dame Henrietta Barnet. Dame Henrietta had been a worker in the slums of the East End of London, and her husband was first Warden of Toynbee Hall. She was averse to pubs and shops but keen on the arts (she founded the Whitechapel Art Gallery) and club houses and churches (one of which she got Lutyens to design). She aimed for a broad mix of social classes though in fact Hampstead was quickly taken over by the middle classes.

The great success of these ventures encouraged every developer to talk of a garden suburb. Few had sufficient land and vision to bring them to perfection, but many tried and trumpeted their ideas. Thus it was in Farnham.

Farnham: Great Austins

South of Farnham railway station in 1900 lay an empty tract of land covered with sand and gravel pits and heathland vegetation. The land was mostly too poor for farming, yet it sloped up to a ridge from which there were fine views of the town, and of West Surrey generally; the Greenhill Ridge was where at one time Tennyson had come to sit, wondering whether to build his house there or on the hill at Aldworth, near Haslemere.[1] It was away from the town and its commercial buildings but very convenient for the railway station. A row of semi-detached red brick villas marched up the slope towards Tilford and Frensham but did not extend more than a few hundred yards from the railway line. The empty land beyond later became known as Great Austins, and was the scene of most of Falkner's early work.

The first developer was the owner of the Farnham Flint, Gravel and Sand Company, Tom Mitchell. He built himself a house called The Lindens (now demolished and replaced by flats) at the junction of Tilford Road and what became a new road created by him (later called Great Austins) which cut though the heathland between Tilford Road and Firgrove Hill. He owned brick and tile works at Crondall, lime works at Seale, potteries in Hale, and a farm further along the Tilford Road called Costleys which later provided building land on the edge of the Great Austins area. He was also a local councillor. So he was well equipped to take advantage of what became a boom area for new housing, albeit that he preferred to sell off building plots rather than attempt to develop it all himself. The only house he built there, apart from the Lindens, was called The Dym.

At about the same time T.W. Sidebotham, the crusading vicar of The Bourne which included the Great Austins area, persuaded the Water Company to lay piped water to the area in order to prevent a recurrence of the cholera epidemic which had ravaged the village in the 1890s.

There was no single overall developer of the Great Austins area. Originally the land was owned by the Farnham Flint, Gravel and Sand Company, but around 1897 they were open to offers for the land from speculative developers. Thus two plots of land in Greenhill Road (the 'best' road in the area) were owned in 1900 by a John Knight of Vernon House (the old house in Farnham's West Street where Charles I spent a night on the way to his execution). He sold them to a developer who in turn sold them on with a stipulation that any house to be erected must cost at least £1,000 and have a belt of trees and shrubs planted along the boundary: one of the resulting houses was Mavins Court (originally called Great Mavins), built as a speculative development by Falkner in 1906. An early map of the area indicates that Falkner and a rival architect, Arthur Stedman, had in fact bought up several plots for development. In Falkner's case this was often in partnership with his friend Charles Borelli.

All developers were concerned to get the best prices. This led them to ensure that the plots of land were big enough to appeal to an upper-middle class type of occupant. The most desirable south-facing plots, on Greenhill Road at the top of the hill, were several acres in size. Even the lesser plots on Great Austins specified a building line of not less than 40 feet (in Greenhill Road it was 50 feet) from the road.

The speculative builders, who saw that the demand for smaller villas had been sated for the moment, were keen to concentrate on a 'superior' type of house in an area of low housing density.

> There was still plenty of money around and enough local tradesmen, hop-growers, brewers, gravel merchants and the like, not to mention the increasing number of wealthy outsiders who sought to live in the town …The southern slope of the valley was, from an estate agent's view, a highly desirable residential area, the higher up the slope the better. 'The higher the fewer' principle was adopted in the years that followed, for the houses which came to be built on this slope grew bigger as you climbed up the steeply rising roads. And the people who built them became richer and richer. The Great Austins and Cobbetts Park [now Leigh Lane] estates on the ridge between the Tilford Road and Frensham Road were the *ne plus ultra* in the local domestic scene. The very field names were impressive—Great Austins and Little Austins, smacking of Augustinian monks.[2]

The roads of the area were formally named in 1912.

The People who lived in the Garden Suburb

Two of Farnham's most famous citizens grew up on the edge of the Great Austins area. The first was William Cobbett, who recalled that he received the rudiments of his education there in the 1760s:

The most interesting thing was a sand-hill which goes from a part of the heath down to the [Bourne] rivulet. At a due mixture of pleasure with toil, I, with two brothers, used occasionally to *desport* ourselves, as the lawyers call it, at this sand-hill. Our diversion was this: we used to go to the top of the hill which was steeper than the roof of a house; one used to draw his arms out of the sleeves of his smock-frock, and lay himself down with his arms by his sides; and then the others, one at head and the other at feet, sent him rolling down the hill like a barrel or a log of wood. By the time he got to the bottom, his hair, eyes, ears, nose and mouth, were all full of this loose sand; then the others took their turn and at every roll, there was a monstrous spell of laughter. I had often told my sons of this while they were very little, and now I took one of them to see the spot. But, that was not all. This was the spot where I was receiving my *education*; and this was the sort of education; and I am perfectly satisfied that if I had not received such an education, or something very much like it; that, if I had been brought up a milksop, with a nursery maid everlastingly at my heels, I should have been at this day as great a fool, as inefficient a mortal, as any of those frivolous idiots that are turned out from Winchester and Westminster School, or from any of those dens of dunces called Colleges and Universities. It is impossible to say how much I owe to that sand-hill.[3]

12 George Sturt, Falkner's contemporary critic.

The second was George Sturt who lived in the adjacent village of The Bourne and wrote several books about the craftsmen and labourers of the Farnham area. In 1911 he wrote *Change in the Village* under the pseudonym of George Bourne, with much sympathy for the poor, proud people of The Bourne.

He told how the new house-owners employed local men from The Bourne to plant and maintain their new gardens, and took in their daughters as maids and cooks. Economically this new employment must have been welcome, but Sturt[4] thought it degrading. 'Middle class domesticity, instead of setting cottage women on the road to middle-class culture of mind and body, has side-tracked them—has made of them charwomen and laundresses [and domestic drudges] so that other women may shirk these duties and be "cultured".' The cottager who used to cultivate his own vegetables was now employed as a gardener:

the things which these people require of him—the wanton things they ask him to do with the soil, levelling it to make lawns, wasting it upon shrubberies and drives, while they fence-in the heath patches and fence out the public—prove to him more fully than any language can do that they put a different value upon the countryside from its old value, and that they care not a jot for the mode of life that was his before they came there. ... the employers most conscientiously humane are those who can least avoid, in their tastes and whole manner of living, snubbing him and setting him down in an inferior place. They cannot help it, now that they have thrust themselves on him as neighbours.

Sturt described the inequalities that ensued, such as the new public health regulation forbidding the keeping of pigs (not unreasonable, but contrary to previous custom—both donkeys and pigs abounded in the area—and affecting the livelihood of the old residents), and the way in which the labourer no longer felt at home there.

> As he sweats at his gardening, the sounds of piano-playing come to him, or of the affected excitement of a tennis party; or the braying of a motor-car informs him that the rich who are his masters are on the road. ... They betoken to all the labouring people that their old home is no longer quite at their disposal, but is at the mercy of a new class who would willingly see their departure. Covetous eyes are upon the valley and the people's position there has grown insecure.[5]

Sturt resented the way in which the original villagers meekly gave way before the affluent newcomers, and was delighted that a parish meeting was successful in squashing a proposal by developers to close the old footpath along Greenhills.

> Several Bourne men went along the next day to clear the path. To them up comes Falkner telling them to stop and accusing them of cutting the young oak trees. But it takes a strong man to deal with a Trusler [a local man admired by Sturt]: "I ent cutting yer trees", he said, "I'm only clearing the path. You better stand clear! I cuts everything that's in the way!" And he flourished his fag hook. "I'll give ye Dippenhall [Falkner's home territory]!"[6]

The footpath survives today, but the indigent cottagers have been replaced by an affluent middle class, keen to stamp a new character on the area. In addition to their new houses, a series of new community buildings have been erected in the new garden suburb of the Great Austins area. Many of these replaced older community buildings in the town centre

In 1906 Farnham Grammar School, Falkner's old school, was relocated to a new building in Morley Road designed in a vigorous blend of Queen Anne and Philip Webb by the County Architects, Jarvis and Richards. In 1911 an Anglican church was built on Swingate Road, replacing an older church (of which the churchyard remains) in Vicarage Lane. This church, St Thomas-on-the-Bourne, was endowed with a big block of land along Swingate Road, which was later sold for housing; it now has a far more affluent congregation than the old Farnham parish church of St Andrew. Near the new church a village hall was built, and on the other side of Firgrove Hill Road a tennis and sports club (the Bourne Club) was established with the very best facilities. On the Tilford Road in 1929 a Catholic church was begun to replace an older church on Bear Lane in central Farnham. This new church, dedicated to St Joan of Arc, was a brick building with a barrel vault and neo-Georgian style designed by the London firm of Nicholas and Dixon-Spain with some input from Falkner, as his friend Charles Borelli was the prime sponsor; after completion in 1937 it was much praised by Arthur Mee.[7] In 1938 a new Girls' Grammar School (now South Farnham Junior School) was built in Menin Way, also on the edge of the Great Austins area; like so many other buildings in the area it is of brick with a Georgian-style entrance and big sash windows.

Middle-class dominance was complete, both in housing and in amenities. Now that the trees and shrubberies and hedges have reached maturity the area has a new form of beauty. In 1982 a Great Austins Preservation Area Group was formed by residents 'to preserve the nature and amenities of the area by monitoring all planning applications and opposing those which might harm or destroy its character.'[8] In 1993 they applied for the long term special protection afforded by Conservation Area status, concerned that 'the latest planning policy guidance on Housing emphasises the need to protect rural and Green Belt areas by concentrating development within urban boundaries. The need for smaller household units suggests that residential areas will remain a prime source by infilling, conversion and re-development.'

Some of this had already taken place—for example Falkner's Great Austins House in the Tilford Road had been converted into flats, some of its fine trees cut down, and a row of smaller houses built in its large garden. When it was built it had featured prominently in the national architectural press: 'The interior is very interesting. The dining room is panelled throughout with Jacobean oak with exposed ceiling joists, and in the drawing room is a frieze modelled by artists of the Bromsgrove Guild of Craftsmen.'[9] Now the only part described in the Waverley Council list of buildings of special interest is the outbuilding at the entrance, which combined the function of stable and dovecote.

The Preservation Group argued that further infilling of plots and felling of trees would be detrimental to the character of the area. In December 1993 the status of Conservation Area was awarded (albeit not to nearby Leigh Lane, which had three important Falkner houses) which strengthened the presumption, in town planning terms, against infilling and demolition and required that any new developments must sustain the character of the area. As in all Conservation Areas, no tree there now may be felled without permission.

Falkner and Great Austins

In his Journals (pp. 869-70) Sturt remarks on his distress at 'the multitude of villas going up—many of them by Harold Falkner … Falkner is, in fact, the evil genius of this countryside … his tasteless replacement of what was once the beautiful, tree-lined, gorse-covered Vicarage Hill.' Sturt knew Falkner, who designed a porch for his cottage, and mentions him in his Journals many times. After his stroke in 1916 Sturt became increasingly pessimistic about the future of Farnham.

Although Falkner was always happy to convert older buildings there was nothing worth his while in the Great Austins area apart from Greenhill Farm, where he rebuilt the old farmhouse in conjunction with a nearby cottage and barn, thereby creating a strip of three houses which have since been further modernised.

Within the Conservation Area as originally proposed by the Preservation Group 20 of the 133 houses are by Harold Falkner, and there is a similar number in the area just outside it. In the period 1903-6 most designs were made under the partnership name of Niven, Wigglesworth and Falkner so it is not possible to say that they were exclusively the work of Falkner, but there is a general presumption that, as his partners had much business outside Farnham and he was the most local member of the firm, they are his work rather than his partners'. Most of the published drawings carry his signature or initials.

Before he joined the partnership the earliest houses he designed were, as one might expect with a young architect just starting out, done for family connections. The first was Strangers Corner for his old Art Master, W.H. Allen. Externally this is in the Wrenaissance style, but internally there are many Arts and Crafts touches. In 1902 he added an extension to provide, as appropriate for an Art Master, a first-floor studio, with a big north-facing window, panelled walls and some (non-structural) ceiling beams. The house is still well preserved today, instantly recognisable from his drawings in the architectural press.

Another of his earlier houses was for his sister, nine years older than him, who had married the local solicitor Richard Mason. This house, in the Arts and Crafts style, is at Shortheath, at the time just outside Farnham but now absorbed within it. The Falkner Arts and Crafts touches are already well-defined—the varied roof line, the bay window, the loggia, the shallow arches over the main internal features, the drawing room with its panelling and inglenook fireplace, the hall with green tiles on the wall and unglazed terra cotta tiles on the floor.

After he joined the Niven and Wigglesworth partnership in 1903 Falkner's career took off with a flourish of houses in the Great Austins area. Altogether the following were illustrated in the architectural press (the date relates to the publication, not the date of completion):

Of his own
 1901 and 1902 Strangers Corner [for W.H. Allen]. Exhibited at the Royal Academy
 1901 Cottage for Mr F. Sturt
 1903 House at Shortheath [for his sister, Mrs Mason]
by the Niven Wigglesworth and Falkner partnership
 1903 House, Lodge Hill [Merlewood]
 1904 Orchard House, 7 Little Austins
 1906 Cottage at Farnham [drawing exhibited at the Royal Academy]
 1906 House on the Great Austins Estate [Great Austins House, Tilford Road]
 1906 Five 'cottages' described in detail in a book by J.H. Elder-Duncan of *The Architectural Review*
 1907 House and Garden at Farnham [Merlewood]
 1907 Mavins Court [Greater Mavins], Greenhill Road [also shown at the Royal Academy]
 1907 Cottage in Farnham [model for Green Tubs, The Packway 1908]
 1909 Bourne Corner [now Shottisham Lodge], Swingate Road
and by Falkner on his own again
 1908 and 1910 Ilona [now Montclare House, Grade II Listed], Greenhill Road

1909 Elm Tree Cottage, 10 Great Austins (for Leo Borelli)
1910 Squirrels, 5, Old Farnham Lane
1911 Leigh House, Leigh Lane [built 1908]
1911 Costleys [now Greenhill Brow], Leigh Lane [built 1908]
1911 Furzedown, 17 Great Austins
1911 70, Firgrove Hill
1913 Three Houses at Farnham [Costleys, Leigh House, Margreig]

Several other Falkner designs for houses outside Farnham were also published in the architectural press at this time. It was rare for such a young architect operating in a small geographical area to have so much press exposure. Falkner built many other houses in the area in the decade up to the outbreak of war in 1914. A pattern emerges of an architect who had become, surprisingly quickly, a leading architect in Farnham, and whose work was frequently featured, along with his sketches and articles on historic towns, in the national press.

NIVEN·WIGGLESWORTH·&·FALKNER·ARCHS

HOVSE·ON·GREAT·AVSTINS·ESTATE·FARNHA'M

13 A Falkner house built for £1,000 in 1906 (now divided, with many more houses built in its garden). This sketch by Falkner appeared in *The Builder's Journal and Architectural Engineer.*

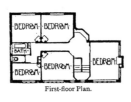

First-floor Plan.

Ground-floor Plan.

After his demobilisation in 1919 Falkner was again in demand to build houses in or near the Great Austins area, and built a further dozen during the next decade, some during his 1927-30 partnership with Guy Maxwell Aylwin. Most of his suburban houses were built in the period 1900-30 but Falkner still had some involvement in suburban Farnham after the Second World War in buying and rebuilding war-damaged houses.

His houses in the Great Austins area are of two types. Some were substantial houses with six or more bedrooms, well built of brick with a regular exterior reminiscent of Wren or Queen Anne. Others were more in the manner of the Arts and Crafts Movement. Common to both were dormer windows, and some oak panelling in the main reception areas. There are also some typical Falkner idiosyncrasies—some items, such as doors or panelling or chimney-pieces, recycled from elsewhere, a slightly awkward treatment of staircases and landings, and the way in which the external appearance is often in conflict with the internal layout such as where internal walls run across windows. The garden was also important—there was usually both a loggia and a bay window overlooking the lawn. The differences between the two types are summarised below.

The 'Wrenaissance' House

- A regular brick facade, the brick being carefully laid, sometimes with ingenious variations such as rustication, use of different colours, alternating headers and stretchers.
- Sash windows (wooden, painted white) regularly spaced. Ground-floor windows have the proportion of a double square; higher windows are slightly smaller but the top-floor dormer windows big enough to avoid sloping ceilings. An occasional round window.
- White painted front door with an elaborate Georgian style porch, sometimes accentuated by pilasters. The front door signalled the taste and importance of the owner.
- A staircase as grand as size of the house allowed, often running across windows.
- Georgian style cornices in the main rooms, and pediments over main internal doors.
- Overall style reminiscent of the early 18th century. Throughout the 20th century this was such a popular style as to be used for a variety of different buildings, from country houses to telephone exchanges. It was also sufficiently anodyne to be used, as Falkner did, for speculative developments.

This was a style which Falkner favoured for his larger houses, several of which were featured in *Country Life* and are described in Chapter 4.

In 1927, just before his partnership with Aylwin, he built Mavins End in Greenhill Road for a former Editor of The Times of India. A grand house in the Wrenaissance style (similar to Montclare House, built by Falkner in the same road), it is especially notable for its garden which he laid out even before starting the building. While the owner was in India Falkner added a brick gazebo without

14 Entrance to The Priory.

even asking for authorisation. Both the house and garden are now Listed Grade II, and are described in more detail in Chapter 5.

The attention to garden layout is repeated in The Priory in Swingate Road (see Fig. 14 and Plate II) which he built in 1930 for an aero-engine manufacturer. Though the house was designed in partnership with G.M. Aylwin, it has typical Falkner touches. The main doors are oak, and there is a grand oak staircase and internal balcony. There are shallow arches between the principal rooms. The exterior symmetry of the Wrenaissance style is paramount, so that windows are regularly spaced even where internal walls are built across windows—a WC and a separate cloakroom share the same window—or result in a window being disproportionately close to the wall of a main reception room; yet the loggia is fully glazed, perhaps at the insistence of the client. Smaller versions in a similar style are Falcon (originally Knole) House in Old Park Lane, Over Compton in Waverley Lane, and 70 Firgrove Hill—all outside the Great Austins area but within Farnham.

Cobbetts (see Plate III), built just before the first World War as a speculative development in Mavins Road, at first seems a small version of the Wrenaissance house, complete with an Ionic columned front door surround salvaged (as was the main mantelpiece) from Georgian Moor Park. But internally the staircase has had to be contorted and lit with an awkward internal window; as at The Priory and Knole House, the external symmetry of the windows is paramount even though they may extend across internal walls.

The 'Arts and Crafts' House

- Rendered walls, hung with tiles on the gables
- Windows irregularly placed—asymmetrical, different sizes, and at different levels. Occasionally an oriel window. Sometimes a lozenge shaped window.
- Casement windows, with wooden frames and leaded panes. Occasional stained glass inserts.
- Steeply pitched sloping roofs, with several planes joining at irregular angles.

- Tall chimneys.
- Front door with Arts and Crafts type carving. Most doors of oak, unpainted, with iron studs. Neither the front door nor the windows are especially accentuated (unlike those in the 'Wrenaissance' houses).
- Stained wooden beams in the main ceilings.
- A fireplace with a brick or tile surround. The main fireplace is the heart of the house.
- Unglazed dark red tiles in the hall and loggia.
- A modest staircase with straight banisters.
- Cottage-style rooms with sloping ceilings within the roof.

Although these houses were often described as 'cottages' they were actually quite large with three reception rooms and several bedrooms. Typical are 17 (Furzedown) and 19 (The Mount) Great Austins (see Plate IV), both described in *The Architects' and Builders' Journal* of 1911 as 'interesting examples of work carried out strictly with a view to economy, and in harmony with the requirements of an average household, yet possessing architectural character.' A special feature in today's context is the treatment of the upstairs landing, spacious and angled to catch the evening sun. Another example of his Arts and Crafts houses, albeit that the walls are bare brick rather than rendered, is 6 Middle Avenue which has a steep roofline and tiny balconies.

One of the more notable is Elm Tree Cottage, 10 Great Austins (see Plate V), built for Leo, brother of Falkner's friend Charles Ernest Borelli and father of the Catholic priest Father Vincent Borelli. Lawrence Weaver of *Country Life* was especially impressed by its economical layout and cost, and the use of locally made green glazed tiles around the fireplace and elsewhere. It is likely that these tiles were made at Absalom Harris' Farnham Pottery in Wrecclesham. They appear in several Falkner houses, as do chimneys and floor tiles which may come from the same source. Like Lutyens, Falkner also sometimes used several layers of tiles in place of lintels over windows and doors.

Several of his Great Austins houses, in particular Orchard House, Bourne Corner and Elm Tree Cottage, have an overall style reminiscent of C.F.A. Voysey, in particular the sweep of steeply pitched roofs, the gabled dormer windows recessed into the roof, the white-painted roughcast walls, the projecting windows, and the spacious upper landings. Like Voysey, Falkner enjoyed adding details of vernacular ornamentation in his interiors.

Voysey had built several country houses nearby—Lowicks at Frensham

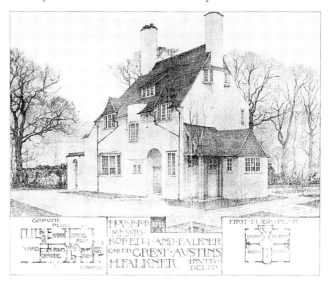

15 Orchard House, Farnham, by Harold Falkner.

in 1894, Greyfriars on the Hog's Back in 1896, Norney Grange at Shackleford and New Place at Haslemere in 1897—though after 1900 his star declined and by 1910 he was reduced to doing wallpaper designs. Falkner told his 1920s partner G.M. Aylwin that Voysey had indeed been his model in many houses, but it was not until the second half of the 20th century that Voysey's work swung back into fashion again. Another influence on his Great Austins designs was C.H.B. Quennell,[10] architect of some fine neo-Georgian houses in Hampstead, of whom Falkner wrote an appreciative obituary.[11] There are traces, too, of the influence of Philip Webb and of Lutyens, both of whom Falkner greatly admired.

As one might expect of an architect who liked old buildings, Falkner was happy to undertake conversions, but there were not many old buildings to convert or adapt in the Great Austins area. He enlarged one old cottage there, and converted Greenhill Farm in Greenhill Road, but this has been since been further enlarged so that few Falkner touches remain. He built and converted several houses in a similar Arts and Crafts style outside the Great Austins area in the period up to the First World War, almost always incorporating some older feature. Typical is Crosslanes near Frensham, built beside an ancient monastery wall and incorporating old panelling supplied by the owner (pictured in *The Builders' Journal* of 29 August 1905).

16 Mavins Court—original design by Falkner.

Adaptation to the later 20th century

Falkner remained always resolutely opposed to Modernism. In the 1930s he was appointed Surveyor to the Crooksbury estate where he strove to keep new building in line with his ideas. *The Architects' Journal* of 19 January 1939 devoted several pages to his correspondence with another architect, Edward Banks, who had a commission to design a house on a site overlooking the golf course. The original design was 'in what, I believe, is called the 'International' or 'Modern' style' but by the time Falkner had finished with it the flat roof had been replaced by a steeply pitched one, some of the windows had glazing bars, and the general effect was 'traditional'.

17 'Architect v. Architect' as illustrated in *The Architects' Journal*, 19 January 1939.

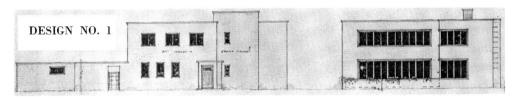

March 7, 1936.

Mr. Banks submitted a first design for a house to the owners of an estate on which his client wanted to build. The owners passed it on to their surveyor, Mr. Harold Falkner.

March 9, 1936.

Mr. Falkner sent the drawing back to Mr. Banks, altered by himself, approved to his amendments. (Design No. 2, below.)

April 7, 1936.

Mr. Banks asked Mr. Falkner if he would approve of grey Dutch pantiles, instead of the red tiles indicated on his alteration.

He further asked him to allow windows free of glazing bars and not as his requirements.

DESIGN NO. 5

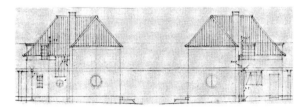

April 29, 1936.

A fresh traditional design was now submitted to Mr. Falkner. Mr. Banks' client was by this time prepared to accept anything Mr. Falkner approved.

Falkner to Banks.   *April 8, 1936.*

Dear Sirs,

         Crooksbury Estates

I have yours of the 7th. I will approve pantiles, the same as Lutyens used at Lambay, provided they are laid same pitch.

I have no objection to the bars in windows being omitted on south front (as a matter of fact, my Client added this objection), on the north and east the view is nothing, and the addition of bars saves money in the case of breakage. Perhaps you will be good enough to let me have a copy of the plan when altered.

         Harold Falkner.

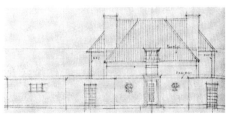

Falkner to Banks.   *May 1, 1936.*

Dear Sir,

         House—Crooksbury Estate

Thank you for your letter and plan of the above, returned herewith, approved.

This is what I call modern without eccentricities. Will you please let me have a print for filing purposes.

         Harold Falkner.

Most Falkner houses in Great Austins are still in single ownership. Now it is a cachet of distinction to have a house designed by Falkner, adding significantly to its value. On the whole the building structures (apart from the Dippenhall houses) have lasted well, since the construction was sound and the layout sensible (albeit with some individualistic quirks which now seem interesting rather than frustrating). Very few Falkner houses have been demolished or radically altered, though some have had their large gardens redeveloped with more housing.

Some houses have been extended skilfully to preserve the original character (The Priory, Green Tubs). Some have neatly been divided into two—Greenhill Brow and Maple House, Mavins End and Mavins House, Buckland House and Robin Hey, Tilford Way and The Beeches. The fact that the larger houses had a separate staircase for servants, to avoid running into them on the stairs, made conversion easier than it might have been. Houses built before 1910, when cars were rare, have had garages added, and a single garage (originally described as a 'motor house') has since been replaced with a garage block for two or more cars.

Internally the changes have tended to reflect the way in which the middle class way of living changed during the 20th century, especially since the disappearance of servants. After the Second World War the kitchen became the key room in the house. The typical Edwardian kitchen suite of several rooms—pantry, larder, scullery, kitchen, coal store—was converted into a single large kitchen in which the owners could eat in comfort and style. Where it was originally positioned to overlook the tradesmen's entrance rather than the garden, it has often been changed to provide a better view of the garden and catch the southerly sun.

The loggia leading onto the garden has been glazed to make a sort of conservatory. On the main bedroom floor larger cupboards have been built in to accommodate the increased amount of clothing which modern affluence promotes; in Falkner's day built-in cupboards were a new development, and rather shallow by today's standards, but at least he provided them, together with more storage space under the eaves. Bedroom fireplaces have been filled in. On the top floor servants' bedrooms have been converted into children's rooms.

Throughout Falkner's life it was quite normal for a prosperous middle-class house of four or five bedrooms to have a single bathroom on the main bedroom floor; the demand for its use was relieved by having a separate WC (and another on the ground floor), wash-basins in each bedroom, and the fact that people did not always bathe daily. The increased emphasis on personal hygiene in the later 20th century required an en-suite bathroom (or two) and separate shower units. As families became smaller it was not difficult to carve these out of existing bedrooms.

Where they were not swept away in post-war enthusiasm for modernisation, the internal fittings are now treasured as Arts and Crafts inheritance: doors and windows with their ironmongery and surrounds, the cornices, wood panelling, the odd stained glass windows, picture rails, and fireplaces (at least on the ground floor). The floors of wood or dark red tiles have been covered (and preserved) by carpets, facilitating a swing in fashion back towards wood and tiled floors.

CHAPTER FOUR

The Small Country House & Country Cottage

The English have long had a love affair with the idea of a house in the country. For at least the past four hundred years the richer people in other countries have aspired to living in a city, but for an Englishman, however rich, to have a place in the country is a main ambition. The idea originated with the landed gentry, but was carried on by the new millionaires of the 19th century who built huge mansions to display their wealth; by this stage the ideal of a house set in large areas of farmland owned by the family was disappearing, but such houses still had extensive stable blocks.

Farnham is unusual in being dominated by no great country house or seigniorial family. The castle which dominates the town has always been owned by the Bishops of Winchester, who also used to own the two elegant 18th-century houses in its parkland—The Ranger's House and The Grange. The closest Farnham gets to a private great country house is Moor Park, where Sir William Temple and his secretary Jonathan Swift lived at the end of the 17th century. Falkner did a fine piece of architectural detective work when he discovered that the stucco facade conceals a brick Jacobean house.[1] He also led the successful campaign to save it from demolition after the Second World War. But neither this house, nor nearby Waverley Abbey nor the large 19th-century mansions at Frensham Heights, Pierrepont or Edgeborough, had any great estate or land-owning family.

As always, the middle classes aspired to the same things as the rich. Because their numbers had increased so much in the 19th century there was an explosion in demand for the country house, albeit with no agricultural land and that the main source of income came from work in the city. The demand was even greater in 1900-14, when Falkner was starting his career, than in the inter-war years when the nation felt less prosperous.

The small country house

The small country house was indeed the staple for many architects at the time when Falkner was starting his career. In a sense it was a delusion, since it was in or near a town rather than in the country. It was part of no landed estate with patriarchal responsibilities, and there were no subsidiary dwellings apart from possibly a single servants' cottage. Privacy was the keynote: in today's terms electrically operated wrought-iron gates with CCTV cameras would be considered an essential. The owners derived their wealth not from agriculture but from investments or pensions or a job with no connection with the countryside.

It was not the residence of the squire. Nor was it the residence of the very rich, whether aristocracy or the new millionaires who might hope to entertain royalty. It was not a place for grand country house parties, nor fox-hunting meets nor shooting parties. The recreations of the owners were (and still are) more likely to be golf on a local club course, or tennis or croquet on a lawn of their house; for the men, billiards in the billiards room, for the women, gardening with the help of a gardener and the latest gardening book. The young people moved around by bicycle, as Falkner and Lutyens did in their 'teens and twenties.

The richer urban middle classes could aspire to the small country house mainly because of the advent of the motor car in 1900, which made horse-drawn transport to the railway station unnecessary. In the South of England the houses were built in 'the Home Counties' within a commuting radius of London. Thus the main outbuilding was a garage, rather than the large range of stables and coach houses in a traditional country house.

Later in the 20th century richer middle-class people aspired to old rectories and farmhouses which could be stylishly refurbished, but in the period 1870-1938 those who could afford it preferred to commission a new country house of their own. The people who lived in these houses often had cultural or intellectual interests as well as money and servants. They were the sort of people described in the novels of E.M. Forster (*Howards End*, 1911) or John Galsworthy (*Forsyte Saga*, 1906-20). They were close enough to London to enjoy the plays of Bernard Shaw, John Galsworthy, and J.M. Barrie (who himself lived on the outskirts of Farnham) and the new 'English countryside' music of Edward Elgar.

The concept of the new-style country house was enthusiastically fostered by the new magazine *Country Life*, which by 1905 had a regular weekly article on a country house. These articles concentrated on great country houses, written in a scholarly fashion by Avray Tipping in the early years and from 1921 onwards by Christopher Hussey who dominated the magazine's architectural writing for many decades. They were illustrated by magnificent black and white photographs taken on full plate cameras by anonymous staff photographers. These articles provide an unrivalled archive on the English country house, arguably one of the greatest of English artistic achievements.

Alongside the main articles on the great country house, *Country Life* started a series on lesser country houses. These were developed by Lawrence Weaver, who had begun his career as a salesman for architectural ironmongery and first contributed to *Country Life* in 1906. He was the magazine's architectural editor from 1910 to 1916, and went on to become a distinguished civil servant knighted for his work on the Empire Exhibition of 1925. He was an admirer of Lutyens and Lorimer and Clough Williams-Ellis, and his articles about their country houses contributed to their successful careers.

I Strangers Corner, Falkner's first new house.

II The Priory.

III Cobbetts, a Falkner design of 1913.

IV The Mount, Great Austins, showing the complex
Falkner gables and Arts and Crafts windows.

V Elm Tree Cottage—the lower left window was originally a porch.

VI Leigh House.

VII Montclare House—carving over the doorway made by Falkner.

VIII Gertrude Jekyll's garden at Munstead, 1900, watercolour by her neighbour Helen Allingham.

IX Farnham Town Hall by Falkner and Aylwin, 1930-33

X Bailiffs Hall, Farnham town centre—Falkner's brilliant reconstruction of Tudor brickwork.

XI Overdeans Court, Dippenhall

XII Burles, Dippenhall

XIII Front door at Grovers Farm, Dippenhall reputedly salvaged from a bank—with Falkner embellishments.

XIV Garden wall at Grovers Farm, constructed in Falkner's magpie style by his tenant David Gillespie.

XV Falkner the versatile.

His reconstruction of the *Goat's Head*.
His drawing of his design for Guildford Cathedral.

He started 'The Lesser Country Houses of Today' series in *Country Life* in 1909 and it continued, not always every week, until 1931. There were many similarities with the important weekly 'Country Homes and Gardens, Old and New' series which featured the ancient mansions of great families, but 'The Lesser Country Houses' series featured the name of the architect rather than the owner. There was a dramatic masthead silhouetting topiary and ancient walls. Although the houses illustrated were generally newly built, the masthead used the most was designed by Arthur Rackham, the leading Edwardian designer of fantasy themes.

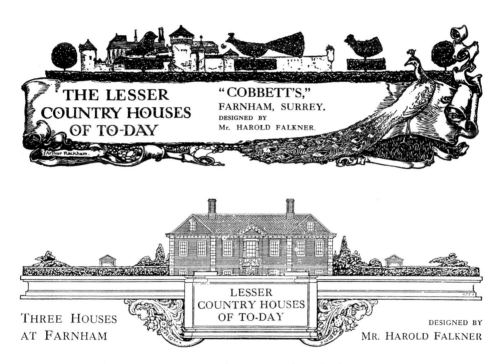

18 *Country Life*'s aspirational mastheads.

Significantly, the first house he wrote about was Red House in Kent, built in 1859 by Philip Webb for William Morris, which had become an icon of Arts and Crafts architecture. Weaver's articles were compiled into books, *Small Country Houses of Today* (Vol. I 1910, Vol. II 1922), which were so popular that *Country Life* commissioned a Volume III by Randall Phillips in 1925. Almost all the houses written about in these books were built in or near towns rather than deep in the countryside.

Weaver was not averse to the use of local architects. Indeed he felt they might have definite advantages over national architects, since they had a better knowledge of local materials, the local vernacular, and local contractors. Falkner was just such an architect; since he supervised the building work personally, and often participated in it himself, it was important that he and his builders had a close relationship..

Falkner's country houses

Farnham, convenient for commuters to London yet surrounded by 'unspoilt' countryside, was ideal for this type of development. The Eastern edge of Farnham provided Falkner with some good sites, well-wooded and situated on or beside hills. He also built some fine country houses near villages a few miles from Farnham.

'A House in Lodge Hill Road' on the edge of Farnham features in *Academy Architecture* for 1903, attributed to Niven Wigglesworth and Falkner and very much in the Arts and Crafts style. The shape of its plan is angled towards a

House, Lodge Hill, Farnham, Surrey, NIVEN, WIGGLESWORTH AND FALKNER, Architects.

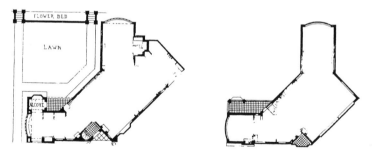

19 An early Falkner design in *Academy Architecture and Architectural Review*.

butterfly shape which enjoyed a popular vogue among Edwardian architects[2] such as E.S. Prior, Detmar Blow, Baillie Scott and Edwin Lutyens; the intention was that this shape would, apart from being different, provide a sun-trap. This house has survived virtually unaltered, not only externally but also with its wealth of Arts and Crafts internal features—downstairs some stained glass windows set in carved stone, ceramic ceilings, frieze of leaves and flowers, and upstairs a large landing and some external balconies.

The shape was again experimented with by Falkner in a vaguely Lutyens-style country house near Thursley which was also shown in the Royal Academy (1907). Falkner's drawing shows an ambitious house for an architect just turned 30 operating in the heart of Lutyens territory. Eighty years later it was further extended.

20 Falkner's design for a house at Thursley exhibited at the Royal Academy 1907.

Subsequently Falkner adopted a more neo-Georgian style for his country houses. All have the characteristic Falkner touches which give the aspects of grandeur and importance which his clients liked: the substantial entrance porch with Georgian-style carving, symmetrically placed sash windows with a dormer row above, the entrance hall opening onto a grand staircase.

Photographs of a long low brick country 'House near Farnham by Niven, Wigglesworth and Falkner' appeared in the *Builders' Journal* of 29 December 1909 and 29 June 1910; it is very much in the neo-Georgian manner, with a flat roof, a loggia on the garden front and a porch on the entrance front. Now called Vere House in The Sands, it has been much altered since and the exterior brick has been coated in stucco; fortunately the latest additions are broadly in keeping with Falkner's original 18th-century intentions. Internally the only unaltered room is the dining room, with a heavy cornice and much panelling.

Country Life of 4 January 1913 featured an article by Lawrence Weaver in the 'Lesser Country Houses of Today' series on 'Three houses in Farnham by Harold Falkner'. Two are in Leigh Lane, Leigh House (see Plate VI) and Costleys (now split into Greenhill Brow and Maple House). Both are surprisingly close to the

21 Costleys, Leigh Lane, Farnham (sketch by Michael Blower).

road for what appear to be very grand houses designed in classical 18th-century manner. This was a usefully bland style since both were speculative developments by Falkner. Costleys is Queen Anne style, with rusticated brick quoins and a small garden gazebo. Leigh House, in the Georgian style (see Plate VI), has a much accentuated entrance doorway and makes use of plaster pilasters which Lawrence Weaver thought rather out of place; the front door and the ironwork over it have been recycled from elsewhere (a common Falkner touch). Both Costleys and Leigh House (and also Sands Lodge opposite, Queen Anne style with a huge hooded entrance door) were built with a separate cottage and 'motor house' for the chauffeur; the other servants had rooms with dormer windows on the attic floor of the main house, accessed by a servants' staircase. The third house is Margreig (later called Fairywood, and now divided into Buckland House and Robin Hey) which is more in the Arts and Crafts style, with casement windows and a big brick fireplace in the hall; clearly it was built for a particular client. All the houses were designed with the principal rooms facing south and west and made use of fine rubbed bricks.

The article is largely repeated in Lawrence Weaver's book *Small Country Houses of Today* (Vol. II, chapter XXVI) except that Margreig is replaced in the text by Ilona, which had been featured in *Country Life* on 3 September 1910. This house, now called Montclare House in Greenhill Road and Listed Grade II, was built in 1908 for a particular client, R.T. Ratcliffe. He had the big straggling staircase built across the hall in order to duplicate the stair at Holland House in Eton where he had been house-master; perhaps he also specified the rather unnecessary shutters on the north-facing entrance front. Falkner designed an especially attractive entrance doorway: the door itself was an old one from France, and the carving above it (see Plate VII) was designed and executed by Falkner himself.

In 1913 Weaver organised a competition for a large new country house in Sussex. 197 entries were submitted by most of the leading architects of the day—including Harold Falkner. The judges were Edwin Lutyens, P. Morley Horder, and Lawrence Weaver. Falkner did not win any of the main prizes but his design was pictured and commented on in an account by Weaver of the results of the competition (*Country Life* supplement, 28 June 1913).

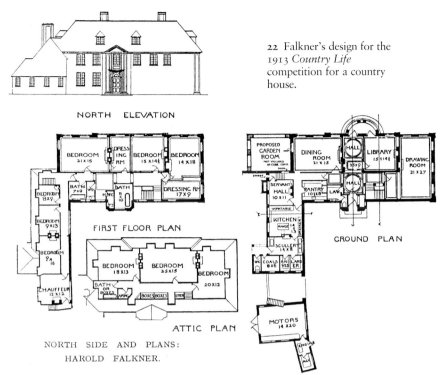

NORTH ELEVATION

FIRST FLOOR PLAN

ATTIC PLAN

GROUND PLAN

NORTH SIDE AND PLANS:
HAROLD FALKNER.

22 Falkner's design for the 1913 *Country Life* competition for a country house.

Typically, Falkner laid out the plan so that all principal rooms faced south, and the north front was mainly taken up with hall, corridors and staircase, WC's and baths, kitchen quarters and servants' bedrooms. Falkner was adept at making his grand houses look grander than they really were, by emphasising their width and height without making them correspondingly deep. In this sense he abandoned the four-room-square box plan of the traditional 18th-century house.

In 1913 Falkner built Tancreds Ford in Tilford for his family doctor, Dr Charles Tanner. Very much in the 'Wrenaissance' manner, it could be easily mistaken for an early Lutyens house (of which there are several in the area). In 1983 it was extended for a new owner, the novelist Ken Follett, by Roderick Gradidge and Michael Blower (see below).

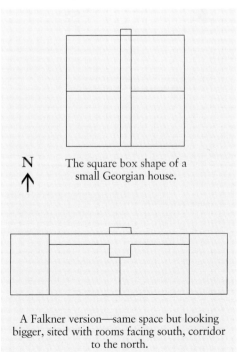

N ↑

The square box shape of a small Georgian house.

A Falkner version—same space but looking bigger, sited with rooms facing south, corridor to the north.

23 Plan shapes for small country houses.

Compton Hill House[3] in Farnham was built just before the First World War on a wooded four-acre site with fine views. Though it appears to be compact, the steeply gabled roof contains five main bedrooms and three servants' bedrooms. The exterior is stucco with a Georgian style porch. There are the usual elements of a Falkner country house—carved front door under a portico, main reception rooms parquet-floored, corniced, and with good chimney pieces. The south-facing loggia overlooks a sea of rhododendrons which would have been very pleasing to Falkner.

Just before the First World War he completed The Chase near Churt, featured in *Builders' Journal*, 19 August 1914, a tall brick house in the neo-Georgian style with an entrance doorway accentuated by pilasters. Though it has since been divided it remains very similar in appearance to Leigh House in Farnham, which must have proved a good investment a few years earlier; unlike Leigh House which is right on the road, it is approached by a long drive, another way of signalling the importance of the owner. Not far away is Hatch Hill House, built at about the same time; firm evidence of a Falkner connection is lacking, but his niece Beryl Falkner attributed it to him and the big Georgian porch and rows of sash windows are typical of the style he favoured at the time.

24 Delarden, Moor Park.

Between the World Wars Falkner built only one new 'country house' in Farnham: this was Delarden built in the late 1930s for the Farnham solicitor, W.H. Hadfield. Or rather, as is often the case, it was built on the instructions of his wife; it was she who reminded Falkner that a WC was needed for guests on the main bedroom floor, and so was a staircase—which he promptly supplied in his typical style, very grand and running awkwardly across the windows of the hall. The house was one of the first on the Moor Park Estate, a private estate of upmarket houses near Farnham developed just before and after the Second World War, and is undoubtedly Falkner's (and the estate's) grandest, designed on a long and narrow plan to make it look even larger than it really is. Falkner took full advantage of the fine southerly views by building in two balconies on the first floor and a big loggia on the ground floor. It has a classical facade of almost perfect symmetry, enhanced by the usual Falkner accentuated front doorway, classical gateway and dormer windows (the dormers and roof above the doorway with a curved pediment), but—unusually for him—the brickwork is entirely covered in stucco. The reason for this (which did not become apparent until renovation in the 1980s) was that Falkner had, in place of his normal high quality local bricks, used cheaper fletton bricks which looked better if rendered. Alas, he also used insufficient lead on the parapets, resulting in water penetration (being on top of a ridge the house is unusually exposed to wind and rain) which released sulphates in the bricks, causing the stucco to crack. The renovation was costly. Nevertheless, like Leigh House thirty years earlier, Delarden retains the appearance of a splendid theatrical backdrop which enhances its neighbourhood. After it was completed in 1938 Falkner withdrew to work almost entirely on his strange houses at Dippenhall.

Falkner country house conversions

Where required, Falkner was always happy to convert older buildings into substantial 'country houses'. With his sympathy for past styles and his talent for making use of old components this was an ideal field for him. Some of the developments were his own speculations and appealed to prospective buyers.

Preservation of old buildings had been a keenly debated issue since the foundation of the Society for the Protection of Ancient Buildings (SPAB) in the late 19th century. The purists felt strongly that anything as historic as a church should not be 'improved', but there was less controversy over more mundane buildings such as cottages and barns. In 1914 Lawrence Weaver published his book *Small Country Houses—Their Repair and Enlargement*. While many of the examples he cited, such as Igtham Mote in Kent and Paycockes in Essex, were substantial medieval houses, he also preached the possibilities of enlarging old country cottages and re-using old barns in keeping with medieval craft traditions. This should involve, he suggested, doing the work in traditional ways, incorporating carved stone and wood, inspired by a sense of historical continuity. This was very much in line with the Arts and Crafts ideals, as espoused by Walter Crane, C.R. Ashbee, Basil Stallybrass—and Falkner himself.

In 1904 he enlarged The Dial House at Millbridge from an old cottage into a six-bedroom country house, making maximum use of the old structure. The client was an artist, Robert Morley, who designed a big 17th-century style sundial for the front of the house, and brought back an ancient wooden front door and chimney-piece from Brittany which Falkner enthusiastically incorporated into the new interior. For many years Falkner dined there on Sundays with its subsequent owners, the Webley family. In 1963 it was owned by Mr Ian Starforth-Hill, Falkner's barrister in his Appeal against conviction for transgressing building regulations in his final Dippenhall house, and Falkner delighted in telling him of its comparatively recent origin.

In 1914 he worked on a late 19th-century country house, Ripsley House near Liphook (geographically the furthest building from Farnham he ever worked on), and his new drawing room with its alcoves for displaying china was featured in *The Architects' Journal* of 18 November 1914 as an example of a new elegance in interior design.

In 1924 Falkner converted three old cottages at North Munstead near Godalming into a mansion for Captain Sampson. Perhaps the Captain, for whom Falkner later built almshouses in Farnham, was introduced to him by Gertrude Jekyll who lived nearby. It was featured in *Country Life* ('Lesser Country Houses of Today' series) of 6 December 1924, and compares well with the many early Lutyens houses in the area. The Victorian trappings were swept away, the old timber beams and trusses were exposed, some big chimneys and a gable were added in the Lutyens style, and various walls of local bargate stone in a matching style—and the result is a convincingly medieval-looking building which is now Listed Grade II. Appropriately, Gertrude Jekyll laid out the garden.

After Falkner's death others were called on to extend his country houses. The acknowledged expert was the architect and historian Roderick Gradidge who wrote the definitive books, *The Surrey Style* and *Dream Houses: the Edwardian Ideal*—and who would have been the best person to write this present book had he not died in 2000. He bounded into Farnham Museum to give a talk on Falkner in 1994, startling the audience first with his pig-tail and tweed kilt, and then with his opening words: 'I know of nowhere else in the world, with the possible exception of the area around Vicenza, where there is such a concentration of fine architecture as there is in the Farnham-Godalming area.'

Unusually for an architect with an original mind, Gradidge preferred to adapt and expand existing houses rather than build new ones, and his adaptations were carefully designed to be in keeping with the originals, but spirited rather than bland. He especially loved the buildings of Lutyens and Falkner, who built, he argued, in 'the natural style for a house—so why bother to look beyond it?' Many of his enlargements of Falkner houses were done in partnership with the help of Michael Blower (Stedman and Blower partnership), the leading Farnham architect of his day and chairman of the Farnham Society and the Farnham Trust. Their work on Tancreds Ford was the subject of two articles in *Country Life*, 17 and 24 November 1983. Their last joint collaboration was on an extension to Overdeans Court in Dippenhall, not completed until 2002.

The country cottage

The country cottage was part of the dream of the English countryside, but meant different things to different people. At one extreme was the sort of labourer's cottage described by Sturt, with no plumbing and a set of just three rooms which could be built for 'a recognised price' of £70. Such were the cottages in The Bourne which Falkner and others were busy replacing with villas for the middle classes. Agriculture in 1900 was going through a period of depression, wages were low and land-owners recognised that any new cottages which were designed for rent must be economical for their developers.

In October 1904 *The Country Gentleman* published an article by its proprietor, J. St Loe Strachey (who was also Editor of *The Spectator*), entitled 'In search of a £150 Cottage' stressing the need for a rigorous approach to building costs per square foot, and suggesting better results might be achieved with modern building methods and designs. This resulted in the Letchworth Cheap Cottages Exhibition of 1905 to which the Niven, Wigglesworth & Falkner partnership contributed a design, as did other leading architects of the day such as Detmar Blow, M.H. Baillie Scott, A.H. Clough and F.W. Troup. The exhibition was a great success, with over 60,000 people attending.

To emphasise that cottages were not to be thought of as a purely rural phenomenon Letchworth organised a second Urban Cottages Exhibition in 1907: the catalogue cover shows a family who do not remotely resemble agricultural workers. By this stage it was clear to men of business that there was more money in catering to middle-class aspirations, and from 1910 the mission of publicising new homes for the middle classes was taken up by the *Daily Mail* with its Ideal Homes Exhibitions.

25 The cover of the catalogue for 1907 Letchworth Urban Cottages Exhibition.

A keynote book on the cottage for the middle-class patron was *Country Cottages and Weekend Homes* published in 1906 by J.H. Elder-Duncan, Editorial Secretary of *The Architectural Review*. Profusely illustrated, it contains examples from all leading architects of the day—including no fewer than five from Niven, Wigglesworth and Falkner (who was actually the key figure), among them the conversion of an older cottage in Ford Lane described below.

As well as writing about country houses, Lawrence Weaver wrote *The Country Life Book of Cottages*, first published in 1913 and reprinted many times. The first edition is sub-titled 'Cottages Costing from £150 to £600'. The second chapter begins: 'For many years the cheap cottage has been the King Charles head of everyday architecture … so many attempts to prove that a reasonable habitation could be built for £150 exclusive of site.' In his book Lawrence Weaver dealt with the whole spectrum of 'cottages', from cheap labourers' cottages, through holiday cottages to eight-roomed cottages with garages and a whole gamut of Arts and Crafts extras. Some of his material came from the *Country Life* 1912 competition for "A Holiday Cottage and Garden for under £550 (plus £150 for the garden layout and £100 for the motor house)". The book begins with cheap cottages for under £175, and progresses through £600 holiday cottages to designs for suburban clusters, as in Hampstead Garden Suburb, where the cottage was part of a much larger complex. Designs were contributed by most of the leading architects of the day, including Lutyens, Baillie Scott, Goodhart-Rendel, and Clough Williams-Ellis.

Two designs by Falkner were illustrated. One was for a cottage costing £315; this had been illustrated already in several architectural magazines, and was finally built in Farnham as The Squirrels, 5 Old Farnham Lane, Great Austins. The other, in the chapter entitled 'The £600 Cottage', was a much more ambitious four-bedroom building with an attached 'motor house' and a complete garden layout.

Most of the designs in Weaver's book were for use in towns rather than for farm workers. All Falkner's cottage designs were developed before the First World War, and built in Farnham suburbia. On the one hand there were the buildings where the main aim was economy combined with a pleasing appearance. Such were the semi-detached cottages he built early in his career on the Ridgway estate, adjacent to but mostly predating the affluent middle-class housing in Great Austins. Their steep roof lines in the shape of an 'M' (of the same shape as his lettering on the Swimming Bath entrance) provide a distinctive feature in an otherwise humdrum road, and have some similarity to the designs of the distinguished C.F.A. Voysey. They are also similar to five pairs of cottages built in Osborne Road, East Farnham, after the First World War although there is no provenance to confirm Falkner's involvement in these.

Writing sixty years later,[4] in 1962, Falkner complained that he

'had bought land on the Ridgway estate and built four houses there as a semi-philanthropic enterprise to let to the working classes (they did work then) at seven shillings a week. There was a clause in the contract—that no house should cost less than £400 to build—that I thought in my innocence was binding on both parties. I was wrong—the Council stepped in and built houses costing £150 each, letting them at 2/6d, [which was] degrading to my tenants at a time of strong social distinction.'

He also designed individual Arts and Crafts cottages for the middle classes. One of his first published drawings was his 1901 Cottage for Mr F. Sturt (Frank Sturt, 1859-1930, bookshop owner, brother of George Sturt and a friend of author Arnold Bennett). As shown in his drawing, the kitchen outlook over the garden is to be separated from the living room aspect by a tall hedge, a surprisingly class-conscious act for such a small house and a client whose family deplored class distinctions. Further sign of middle-class aspirations is the provision for expansion at a later date. In 1906 the Royal Academy exhibited his design in a similar style for a Cottage in Farnham, which stands today in urban surroundings in West End Grove, where Frank Sturt eventually settled, looking much the same as it did a century ago.

In 1903 Falkner bought the old Stream Cottage in Ford Lane, beside a river ford in The Bourne village about which Sturt wrote so much. He lived there himself for several years, and his conversion of the old building was featured in

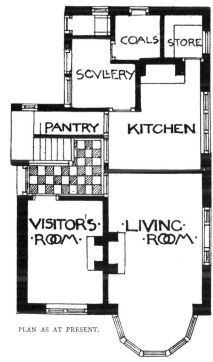

PLAN AS AT PRESENT.

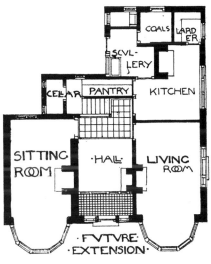

COTTAGE FOR MR. F. STURT, FARNHAM.

We give ground plan and elevation of this cottage, designed by Mr. Harold Falkner; also plan showing building completed by future extension.

26 An early Falkner design in *The Architectural Review*.

27 A superior cottage design exhibited at the Royal Academy (since built in West End Grove, Farnham).

Elder-Duncan's book. He skilfully modernised it, providing extra windows and an extension without losing the original character, retaining the old ironstone garden wall and outbuildings, and embellishing the garden terrace with a pergola.

A Falkner drawing of a Cottage in Farnham, published in the *Builders' Journal*, 17 July 1907, was a speculative design which he built later as Green Tubs [Windycroft] in The Packway. It was extended in the 1990s to make a substantial house but without losing the Falkner appearance and Arts and Crafts ambience. By 1907 Falkner had given up on the idea of designing cottages for the working class, and the 'cottages' he was designing were all suburban houses for the middle class. This was more profitable, and there were plenty of prospective clients in the 'garden suburb' areas of Farnham.

28 A Falkner design of 1907, featured in *The Builder's Journal and Architectural Engineer*.

CHAPTER FIVE
Falkner and Domestic Garden Design

Falkner was not by nature a gardener or garden designer, but he lived through a period of intense public debate about garden design and became a close friend of Gertrude Jekyll. He eventually came to be something of a garden designer himself—and an expert on rhododendrons. In his formative years the subject was dominated by three or four people, two of whom he was very close to, and all of whom were very influential on his own thinking. His own ideas reflected the evolution of English garden design in his lifetime. Above all, he adopted the idea that the house should be united with the garden in one harmonious whole.

William Robinson (1838-1935)

William Robinson was an irascible Ulsterman who dominated the field of domestic gardening in the last quarter of the 19th century. Though a self-educated man who had begun life as a hired gardener he was very opinionated. Emigrating to England in 1861, he worked for the Royal Botanical Society in Regent's Park and was elected to the Linnaean Society at the age of twenty-nine.

In 1871 he founded the weekly magazine *The Garden*. It quickly came to dominate the new field of gardening magazines and he edited it for 25 years. His book *The English Flower Garden* was first published in 1883 and for the next fifty years was the bible of English amateur gardeners.

He was a man of strong opinions which he did not hesitate to express, though in the course of his long life they sometimes changed. He hated elaborate Italian gardens and parterres, topiary work and broad straight gravel paths, the custom of bedding out rows of annuals before flowering and then removing them later. All these were features which required a large garden staff, which his mainly middle-class readers did not command, and preaching against them contributed to his popularity. On the other hand he liked wild and woodland gardens, which were more easily maintained. He loathed the idea of architects being involved with garden design, which he felt should be left to real gardeners.

When he became rich he bought a large country house and invited Edwin Lutyens to advise him on building. But Lutyens disliked him—'He bores me he is so cross and idiotic and anything he does is wrong. He is to deal with exactly like a jibbing horse and it does tire me getting him along.'[1] As a plantsman himself, he was deeply interested in new botanical specimens imported from other countries and continents, especially where they could be grown without greenhouses. New hardy shrubs from Asia such as azaleas, camellias, rhododendrons and magnolias were of great interest; so were alpine plants. For him, a major reason for a garden was that it enabled people to enjoy plants which they would not normally experience. Yet at the same time he was adamant that the landscape should seem to be naturalistic. Falkner was a regular reader of *The Garden*, quickly adopted his passion for rhododendrons, and always incorporated herbaceous borders into his gardens.

Reginald Blomfield (1856-1942)

Many of William Robinson's ideas were opposed by Reginald Blomfield, the eminent London architect under whom Falkner trained. His book *The Formal Garden*, published in 1892 and quickly reprinted with a riposte to William Robinson's criticism, was a plea for the establishment of a formal garden as a proper setting for a house.

Coincidentally, one of the early formal gardens quoted by Blomfield had been established in Farnham at the end of the 17th century. This was Moor Park where Sir William Temple had laid out a garden on Dutch lines, with clipped trees and straight canals. By the 19th century it had disappeared but Falkner became aware of it through his historical investigations into the house.

As an architect himself, Blomfield was in favour of the idea that the architect 'should be free to design the gardens which surround the house as freely and as naturally as he would design the house'. He argued for a re-appearance of garden architecture—bridges, gazebos, balustrades, stairways, walls (of brick rather than stone)—all of which had been banished by the naturalistic landscape gardeners.

Like William Robinson he hated the big parterres with bedded-out flowers and rows of statues favoured by mid-Victorian millionaires, and he was much in favour of grass lawns which the invention of the lawn-mower in the mid-19th century had made more practicable to maintain. But unlike Robinson he favoured artificial garden features such as fountains, dovecotes, sundials, and individual statues (of lead rather than marble, which he felt was un-English).

After many years of vitriolic public debate Blomfield and Robinson became friends in the 20th century, and Blomfield visited Robinson at his country house Gravetye Manor in Sussex. By then a synthesis between their views had been brought about by Gertrude Jekyll, often working with Edwin Lutyens. When Falkner first visited her garden at Munstead Wood he was struck by the way in which 'it was partly formal, partly controlled wild'. Later he recalled the way she related 'with great glee the fact that Robinson designed a garden all squares [Gravetye], and Reggy a garden on a cliff with not a straight line in it [Point Hill]'.

Falkner himself did not adopt Blomfield's ideas as readily as one might expect from a pupil. He built gazebos and pavilions and terraces in his larger gardens, but he worked more closely with Gertrude Jekyll.

Gertrude Jekyll (1843-1932)

Gertrude Jekyll grew up in the Surrey countryside, but her early interests focused on the arts. She finished her education at the South Kensington School of Art where she met Ruskin and Morris and imbibed the philosophy of the Arts and Crafts pioneers. Her early interests were painting and handicrafts, especially embroidery. When she was 25 the family moved to Wargrave in Berkshire but she pined for south-west Surrey, and was delighted to return there with her widowed mother in 1877 to buy land for a house at Munstead near Godalming.

By then she was aged 33 and her eyesight had become too poor for embroidery, and was failing even for water-colours. She turned increasingly to gardening, which she viewed as a form of painting, and writing about gardening for the new gardening magazines. Her plantsmanship, her practical approach and her talent for writing made her immensely popular among the growing number of middle-class readers, many of whom were women,

Varieties of 'natural' gardens popularised by Gertrude Jekyll were woodland gardens, wildflower gardens, cottage gardens, fruit gardens, and rock gardens. Her greatest speciality was the planning of herbaceous borders, a concept first introduced by William Robinson. These became such a common feature of early 20th-century English gardens that it is difficult to realise how new a concept they were in late 19th-century garden design. They involved long rectangular beds with flowering plants grouped 'naturally' rather than in rows, and with delicate colours shading into each other rather than in vivid and contrasting hues; the plants were perennials intended to be permanent features rather than, as had been the custom in great houses, annuals to be planted out when about to flower and removed when flowering was over.

Because of her failing eyesight she preferred to group plants in clumps, and did this in a way one might expect from a painter. She held that "Planting ground is painting a landscape with living things". She liked old-fashioned and native plants, and was especially keen on lilies and roses and water-plants, but her real talent was for designing and writing about gardens. In 1881 she started writing for *The Garden* magazine, and was soon a major contributor. In 1900 Edward Hudson, the *Country Life* founder, invited her to become joint Editor of *The Garden* with E.J. Cook who had edited Ruskin's Works. She shaped her articles into several best-selling books—*Wood and Garden* (1899), *Home and Garden* (1900), *Lilies for English Gardens* and *Wall and Water Gardens* (both 1901). She was the co-author, with Lawrence Weaver, the *Country Life* architectural editor and admirer of Lutyens and Falkner, of *Gardens for Small Country Houses* 1912 (later reprinted as *Arts and Crafts Gardens*).

The English Garden as a Tradition

By 1900 the English garden had become a new tradition,[2] invented, like the English Christmas and Scottish kilts, to bolster national identity through providing links with an imaginary past. It presented a reassuring image of Englishness at a time when the old order was being challenged by socialism at home and by American and German economic power abroad. In particular the English cottage garden, as written about by Gertrude Jekyll, Rudyard Kipling and Henry James, was portrayed as a safe haven wherein Englishness was nurtured. No matter that English cottage gardens had more often been used by cottagers for pigs and chickens and kitchen vegetables; they could also be seen as the home of native flowers such as foxgloves and primroses, honeysuckle and rambler roses. Kipling's poem 'The Glory of the Garden' was a comforting myth to turn to in the face of industrialisation and trade unionism, and buttressed the virtues of hard work:

Our England is a garden, and gardens are not made
By saying, Oh how beautiful, and sitting in the shade.

For gardens of this sort it was essential that they appeared to be natural and have roots deep in English history. Thus traditional flowers like hollyhocks and phlox and rambler roses were favoured, and foreign and regimented flowers avoided. Herbaceous borders, new invention though they might be, fitted in well. So did the arts and crafts idea of dividing the garden up into 'rooms' rather than have the grandiose vistas favoured in earlier times.

The late 19th century witnessed a wave of popular watercolour painters of gardens, many of whom lived in south-west Surrey. Myles Birkett Foster settled in Surrey in 1863 and was buried at Witley in 1899. Helen Allingham (1848-1926) also lived at Witley, near Gertrude Jekyll, and was a close friend of hers (see Plate VIII). Randolph Caldecott (1846-86) moved to Frensham from where he used to visit Edwin Lutyens' parents at Thursley, and is credited with first turning the young Lutyens' thoughts to architecture. Walter Tyndale had a house built in Haslemere in 1906. All these, and Kate Greenaway (1846-1901), were greatly admired not only by the Arts and Crafts Movement but also by the populace at large. They stimulated a nostalgia for rural crafts and gardens, which was further fuelled by Gertrude Jekyll's writings and researches.

One of the most important texts, reflecting the strong interest she shared with Lutyens in the Surrey vernacular, was Jekyll's *Old West Surrey* (1904). Englishness was a characteristic of the work of Lutyens and Jekyll, and of Falkner himself, all of whom had grown up in the same corner of south-west Surrey and admired the same farm buildings and cottage gardens.

Gertrude Jekyll and Edwin Lutyens

By 1889 Gertrude Jekyll was a stout spinster with a considerable reputation for her gardening writings and a wide range of contacts among the rich for her talents in garden design. At a tea-party at the home of Harry Mangles, who lived near both of them at Littleworth Cross, Seale near Farnham, she first met the young Edwin Lutyens. Lutyens was invited because he was building a gardener's cottage for Harry Mangles, brother-in-law of his first patron Arthur Chapman. Jekyll was there because Mangles had a passion for rhododendrons—a shrub on which Falkner himself later came to be an expert. Mangles was one of the earliest connoisseurs, having lived near native rhododendron country to the north of Bengal, and had no qualms about introducing non-native species.

As Lutyens recounted later, 'the silver tea kettle and conversation reflected rhododendrons' but she did not speak to him until she was leaving, when she invited him to tea at Munstead. He cycled up to her house the following week

29 Sketches by Lutyens of Gertrude Jekyll as angel (left) and as young architect's mentor (right).

dressed in his best clothes and full of apprehension. At this point she was 45 and he was aged 20. It was the start of a lifelong friendship. They spent many afternoons driving around West Surrey in her pony cart sharing their interest in vernacular buildings and artefacts, an interest which bore fruit some years later in her book *Old West Surrey*. Falkner wrote to Jekyll's biographer Betty Massingham: 'Miss Jekyll had ... a knowledge of the very finest building techniques which she transferred to Lutyens, and that 'sense of materials' made him different from all other architects of his time.' The young Lutyens was an entertaining companion, full of schoolboy humour and adept at charming those he wished to influence; he introduced his fiancée Emily Lytton to her and they had many jolly evenings together at Munstead.

Jekyll asked him to design her new house at Munstead Wood. Even before it was finished she was delighted and lost no opportunity of showing it off to her rich friends. Soon Lutyens, never slow to follow up a lead, had commissions to build several large houses in the area, including Orchards at Munstead and Fulbrook House at Elstead. He asked her to design gardens to surround his houses, and the Lutyens-Jekyll combination achieved lasting fame as an example of how an architect and a gardener might work together to create a harmonious whole in which a new house blended perfectly with its setting. Of some 300 gardens which she designed, over 100 were in collaboration with Lutyens. Together they elevated the English garden into a new form of national aesthetic. Their greatest joint triumph was Deanery Garden in Berkshire, designed for the influential Edward Hudson, founder of *Country Life*. Lutyens' biographer Christopher Hussey wrote: 'Deanery, at once formal and irregular, virtually settled that controversy of which Sir Reginald Blomfield and William Robinson were protagonists, between formal and naturalistic garden design. Miss Jekyll's naturalistic planting wedded Lutyens' geometry in a balanced union of both principles.'

From the architectural point of view the characteristic of this approach was the way in which the house merged with the garden via loggias and terraces, and the garden was adorned with architectural features such as flights of steps, sunken gardens, pools, walls and clipped hedges. In order to look 'natural', highly artificial features such as temples, balustrades and rows of statues were to be avoided. Theoretically this approach required less labour and more sympathetic thought by the man or lady of the house, but actually it could be quite labour-intensive: moving mowing machines between terraces, or clipping long hedges, was a major chore before the invention of modern machinery; within two years of Gertrude Jekyll's death Lutyens was bemoaning the way in which her Munstead garden was collapsing without the attention of her 11 gardeners (actually there were only five, of whom two looked after the vegetables).

As explained by Muthesius in 1904: 'The garden is seen as the continuation of the rooms of the house … a series of outdoor rooms, each of which is self-contained and performs a separate function … [thus] the garden must extend not just to one side of the house but all around it, so that the house seems from all angles to rest on an adequate base.'

By the end of the 19th century Lutyens had moved his home and office to London and become established as a prominent architect. At this stage Gertrude Jekyll may have felt the lack of a local young man, which is where Harold Falkner came in.

Gertrude Jekyll and Harold Falkner

Harold Falkner first visited her at Munstead in the summer of 1900, toiling up to her house on his bicycle as Lutyens had done a decade earlier. It was a hot day: the handlebars of his bicycle were almost too hot to hold, and he sweated in his high collar, straw boater, Norfolk jacket and tapered knickerbockers. But she took a liking to him and every month for the next thirty years she summoned him by postcard to visit her at Munstead. In 1900 she was aged 56 and Harold was aged 24. She had been well-known via her writings for many years, and attracted many more visitors than she wanted. Why did such a friendship begin between a middle-aged spinster and a young and unknown bachelor?

Harold is sometimes described as the godson of Gertrude Jekyll, but there is no evidence of this. There is no mention of Gertrude Jekyll on the record of Harold's baptism at Bramley church, where he was christened by the vicar of Bramley, the Reverend Henry Power, on 2 January 1876, though it was not usual at that time for the names of godparents to be included in the baptismal register. One might expect a godson to receive a legacy from his godmother, but there is no mention of Harold Falkner in Gertrude Jekyll's will. Godparents are usually family friends chosen in the first year of a child's birth, but there is no evidence that the Falkner and Jekyll families knew each other then. The Jekylls, who lived at Bramley for many years, left for Berkshire two years before Harold's mother moved to Bramley and gave birth to Harold. Possibly the older Falkners, who farmed at Dippenhall, might have known Gertrude Jekyll's maternal grandmother, Emily Thomson, who was the daughter of John Poulett Thomson of Waverley and lived in Farnham—but this is a very tenuous speculation. It was never alluded to by Harold's niece Beryl, who specifically denied that Gertrude Jekyll was his godmother.[3] It is more likely that the term *godson* was used in a half-humorous way, the sort of joke that Harold used to play—such as when asked the date of his birthday he would often reply 'April 1st' or 'Same day as Churchill.[4]'

Probably Harold was introduced to Gertrude Jekyll by a mutual friend; this is most likely to have been his architectural mentor Reginald Blomfield, though it might have been Lutyens, who was an acquaintance, or his old art tutor W. H. Allen, whom Jekyll would have known through the South Kensington School of Art and the Arts and Crafts movement. Harold himself wrote: 'She had a sort of respect for architects, and over-rated them considerably as a class. Probably she took Lutyens as her standard and thought that all his colleagues would be as interesting if not as entertaining'.

Perhaps when Gertrude Jekyll befriended the young Falkner she was trying to recapture some of the pleasure of the early days of her friendship with Lutyens. But Falkner did not have the same schoolboy sense of fun, nor was he able to provide the connections which she liked with rich or aristocratic people (apart from the snobbish attraction, big design jobs paid better than small ones). She never promoted his architectural career, and he seemed to be content to visit her, when summoned, in order to learn more about gardening. Their correspondence was always on the formal basis of 'Dear Miss Jekyll'.

His recollections of her are a valuable source for her biographers. Betty Massingham, who wrote the first major non-family biography, *Miss Jekyll: Portrait of a Great Gardener* (1966), quotes freely (as I have done in this chapter) from his 1963 letters to her. She acknowledged the great debt she owed him as a biographer—but never refers to him as Jekyll's godson. Falkner liked and admired Gertrude Jekyll as a person, and his descriptions of her, written when he was over eighty, are complimentary. His powers of recall, when writing forty, fifty or sixty years later are amazing, testifying to the impression she made and to his own memory:

'She combined the energy of an ant, the perseverance of a spider, the unwavering pursuit of an idea, undeterred by a thousand failures and uninfluenced by any outward tendency she did not choose to notice.

'I believe some people found GJ autocratic. To me she seemed the most modest and meekest of gardeners. She was never tired of telling of her failures with onions and would even admit that anemones and phlox were nearly heartbreaking.

'She was the complete vanquisher of all her adversaries. ... That anyone with her magnificent urbanity could have an adversary may seem absurd, but it was so. She could differ decidedly, promptly and completely, and she was sometimes not in the least disinclined to show it.

'Someone, somewhere has talked of 'a little old lady'. G.J. was not little bodily or in any other way. She must have been, when I first knew her, some five feet ten and weighed ten or twelve stone; with rather a deep voice but not at all masculine, without the slightest gush, capable of considerable tenderness, always putting people at their ease or keeping them there, always thinking, contriving, giving or storing information.

'She differed from all other gardeners in the fact that she was an artist. Gardening was not a craft or even a science to her—it was an art.'

He introduced the Secretary of the Royal Horticultural Society to her, and they tried, without success, to raise the question of the future of her garden after her death.

'The Secretary had been prompted and did his best. We talked of future developments of the R.H.S., preservation of gardens, the importance of design, even colour in the garden (a very favourite subject), but the future of Munstead Wood was evidently not to be discussed, and it may have only been a co-incidence but it was two months before I received my next postcard to "come again".'

In contrast to Lutyens, who rarely visited her in old age, Falkner remained fond and faithful to her commands until the year of her death.

Falkner's Views on Gertrude Jekyll's Garden Designs

In his letters to Betty Massingham (which she quotes in her Jekyll biography) Falkner provided some perceptive eye-witness descriptions of the house which Lutyens had built for her in 1896 and the garden she had created around it.

'In her first books she seemed to harp on naturalism in gardens in direct opposition [to the ideas of *The Formal Garden*] but gradually she and Lutyens came to our [i.e. Reginald Blomfield's] way of thinking and from the second addition of Crooksbury on to Great Maytham had become Formal in garden and classic in houses.'

In fact, the Jekyll gardens were a blend of the formal and the natural, where to be 'natural' required artifice and planning.

'Munstead Wood had one considerable peculiarity. The entrance was through an arched opening in a wall in a stone-lined corridor, with a view of the pantry or the larder on the left which generally raised in the uninitiated some doubt as to whether it was the front or the back door. Everything was always dead quiet. The bell may have made some sort of tinkle or buzz at its other end, but the result at the operating end was nil until the door opened ...

'My introduction to Munstead Wood garden was a disappointment because (a) I did not then know enough about gardening to appreciate it, (b) I was not sufficiently an artist to understand restraint.

'In February, an early pyrus or two might be showing colour. There are trim box hedges, Horsham stone and sanded paths, the grass is still brownish-grey past the formal lily pool and big clipped box hedges, brownish and dormant, down the nutwalk—perhaps one or two would have broken out into their catkins—the ground underneath clothed with a green fern in spring leaf and in and among these the glorious hellebores, greenish-white and cream, purple to nearly black, and brick red to pick up all the blends and colourings. How long they lasted or what hybridising had gone into their constitution I do not know, but they went on gradually becoming greener until primroses and anemones and a few pale daffodils filled their place.

'It is to be noted that G.J.'s favouring of this colour scheme was almost exactly William Morris's; purples and brick reds shading into white on a green and white patterned ground. And so round the back of the summerhouse into the spring garden and here the scheme varies from year to year, but generally begins with bluish-white arabis, scillas and muscari (heavenly blue and the darker one) to creams of double arabis, alyssium citrinum with tall tulips used as spots, but never any but white and yellow. The flaming reds were used farther on where, on favourable occasions, a setting sun shone and burned like the reds in old glass, but whether this was art or artfulness I never could quite determine.

'Once, soon after the war, the spring garden blossomed out into a fearful and wonderful scheme of purple honesty on a yellow and green background, but I am not sure that I or anyone else was supposed to notice it.

'Later on this part of the garden relapsed into dullness for the rest of the year except for paeonies.

'In the woodland a little later the dog violets would be the centre of attraction—not perhaps a big clump but making an exquisite picture. The wood had three divisions—the silver birches with one of the original large Scots firs used as a focal point towards the purple vista; the chestnuts with their appropriate undergrowth; the heath garden under the firs, and the rhododendrons separated entirely from the azaleas. Daffodils were dispersed throughout the wood, separated into their principal categories but still blended somewhat into one another.

'The polyanthus (Munstead strain) were in the oak wood, the oak stems being bare to a considerable height, giving, at the time the primroses were at their full glory, a faint greenish light from the young oak foliage, which afterwards developed into a fairly deep shade by the time the oak had attained its complete leaf.

'The azaleas had at that time become large, well-developed bushes, all planted with extreme care as to their colour scheme and blending into one another, so that there was never an effect of excessive colour and always a most adorable smell … They were grown between the chestnuts so that the dropped leaves formed a carpet when they came into flower (besides a mulch) so that the whole colour—russets of the fallen chestnut leaves, a few purple heathers, and the creams, golds, oranges, reds and back to pinks and whites— made a perfect scheme.

'The main colour scheme of the June garden was purple geranium, white oriental poppies, sages and lavenders, with a secondary scheme of lupins and irises. Lupins have been since developed by Mr George Russell, and have achieved some notoriety and brilliance, but I do not think they were ever better grown than in this border, particularly Munstead blue which was probably a species, with very large fat flowers of forget-me-not blue and medium spikes, and Munstead white, which was really a cream with white wings and thick petalled bells.'

Though unimpressed by Lutyens' first country house (before its extension) at Crooksbury near Farnham, Falkner came to admire him greatly, both as an architect and as a collaborator with Gertrude Jekyll. He described his first visit to one of their early joint ventures:

'More or less by accident I saw the garden of Millmead, at Bramley. It was June. I had been accustomed to gardens which were only just beginning to promise in June. I was struck 'all of a heap'. I have never seen anything before, nor since, as perfectly developed, so exquisite in every detail, so much in so small a space. Weaver and G.J. subsequently wrote a detailed account of the whole plan ... a very worthy and painstaking account, but it was as nothing to the effect on me.

'In colour, texture, form, background, setting, smell and association—time of day about six on a June evening—it was perfect. It was to me the work of a fairy or wizard, and I had found it right under my nose within a few hundred yards of the house in which I was born, but till then absolutely unknown to me. Since then I have come to know its author more intimately than any other colleague. I have seen many of the great gardens in this country and I have never had the least inclination to alter this opinion. (By the word 'association' I mean that it was English—typical of the English village; owing something perhaps to a hundred foreign influences, but having so absorbed them that their origin is lost and they have become our own).'

Falkner noted that Jekyll 'naturally liked doing big gardens—they paid better and she was always hard up—but it was to the struggling small gardener she appealed.' Falkner himself was such a gardener.

Gardens for Falkner's houses

Like Gertrude Jekyll, Falkner first thought of gardens as an artist, and only later became determinedly practical. He embraced the Arts and Crafts ideal, as preached by Jekyll and Lutyens, that the house must relate to its setting, and that both must relate to English traditions. The Jekyll records contain papers for three gardens planned by her specifically for Falkner. Significantly, their correspondence is on a strictly business level with no hint of a godmother relationship.

The first was Hall's Cottage in Frensham (1923/4), where Falkner was engaged by Borelli's company to combine and enlarge two old cottages into a larger whole (now called Hall's Place). Jekyll's herbaceous border and the stone flagged path are still there, and the yew topiary and hedges have grown to maturity, but the site is now much more remarkable for its architecture. The entrance is dominated by a stone Jacobean gateway taken by Falkner from an old manor house near Reading, and Falkner's extension to the cottages is in impeccably Tudor style.

The second was Mavins End in Farnham which is unusual in that the garden was laid out three years before the house was built in 1927. This was at the instigation of the client, E. G. Pearson who was living in Bombay as managing director of the *Times of India*. Falkner wrote to Gertrude Jekyll:

'I want you to design a herbaceous border for my best garden ... as per my plan and section attached. ... The border can be made up with any kind of earth from pure sand to stiff brick earth. I have a certain amount of leaf mould and enough well-rotted manure. ... I can assure you that the border will remain as designed for some years.'

30 Early Falkner drawings in *The Artist*, 1901.

The site slopes away naturally to the south-west. This slope Falkner divided by a tall stone embankment below which there was a flag-stoned terrace, three curved rectangular pools, and two round pools under the stone wall; the upper and lower levels were connected by stone steps, the centre flight very broad and the side ones curved. At each end of the lower terrace (now sadly divided by the house being split into two) was a brick pavilion with its roof on the side facing the pools supported by Corinthian pillars; above the west pavilion there is an octagonal Georgian-style brick gazebo under a domed tiled roof. Falkner made the most of

FOR·WINTER·CAME·AND·THE·WIND·WAS·HIS·WHIP·

31 Falkner's fairy-tale gardens—Summer and Winter.

the splendid views by incorporating in the house design several upstairs balconies and pillared loggias opening onto the garden on the south and west sides.

The client wrote delightedly:

> I can hardly pay a greater tribute to the architect than by saying that there is no detail in either house or garden that I would wish to change in any way. From the house, which is dignified, well-proportioned and restful, a flight of steps leads to a terrace where long pools reflect the brilliant colours of flower beds and are bright with water lilies and the glint of goldfish. There are sloping lawns, wide flower beds, banks of rhododendron and many other flowering shrubs, and near the house is a "wild" corner—the original land with the pine trees and heath so typical of Surrey.

The house, which is in Greenhill Road, Farnham, is now Grade II Listed both for the building and for the garden. Gertrude Jekyll's original herbaceous border has been demolished to make way for a bungalow next-door, but the architectural features of the garden remain and are enhanced by mature yew hedges. It is a fate typical of Jekyll gardens that, since they involved mainly flowers rather than trees, they have to be re-created every generation—but the yews go on for ever.

Yews, slow-growing but long-living, had an ancient pedigree. In Saxon times they marked churchyards; in medieval times they provided the best wood for longbows; in Stuart times they offered scope for the new fashion of topiary. Perhaps it was this historical background which contributed to the fascination of Rossetti and Morris with yew hedges and topiary, and thus made them a feature of Arts and Crafts gardens: regular clipping could hardly be viewed as naturalistic, but at least it was more natural than the statues and balustrades of mid-19th-century gardens. Thus clipped yew was a feature of Jekyll and Falkner gardens, giving them an architectural quality and enduring much longer than the herbaceous borders.

The third Falkner house for which Gertrude Jekyll designed a garden is Munstead Place, possibly the only architectural commission which he ever got through her, since it was for her neighbour Captain Sampson.

Falkner learned much from Jekyll, but usually designed gardens for his houses without formally engaging her help. He recognised early on the importance of laying out a garden in advance of the house, and paying particular attention to the subsoil. Many of his houses in Great Austins were sited around old gravel pits; an article in *Country Life* describes how at Cobbetts he had to drain away the water, take out the gravel, and enrich the soil with leaf mould.

Standard components of Falkner gardens are rhododendrons and azaleas, quick-growing trees such as chestnuts and willows, lily ponds, a tennis or croquet lawn, an herbaceous border, several rose beds, a pergola, a sundial; all overlooked by a loggia built into the side of the house. In larger gardens he built a gazebo or garden house, usually with classical pillars on one side, where the owners could take tea while surveying the garden. All these elements are present in the plan for the Cobbetts garden. Following the Lutyens-Jekyll pattern of trying to unite the house with the garden, the architecture was extended into the garden by stone

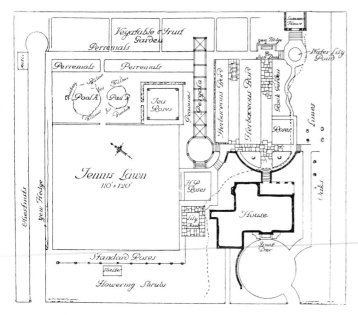

32 Falkner's garden layout for Cobbetts, 1913. The tradesmen's entrance is separated from the front door by a curved wall.

walls and pools and pergolas, and the garden extended into the house by means of climbing plants on the walls—rambler roses were especially popular—and the loggia. If space permitted there was also a fruit and vegetable garden, the need, or at least the economics, for which virtually disappeared after the Second World War.

Rhododendrons were his special interest. 19th-century Britons were avid hunters of new plant species from Asia and America, plants which were later hybridised and adapted for planting in Britain. The rhododendrons brought from the Himalayas by Joseph Hooker in the mid-19th century were particularly exciting as not only did they have splendid blooms but also they readily adapted to British conditions: they took especially well to the poor sandy soil of Surrey. So well, in fact, that they posed a philosophical problem for lovers of the traditional English garden: should they allow it to be invaded by a non-native species whose rampant growth threatened a take-over? In fact they proved their worth by helping to disguise the rash of house-building which spread across the county in the 20th century. Falkner established his own rhododendron nursery in Dippenhall. Wherever soil conditions permitted, and the sandy soil of the Farnham area provided ideal conditions, he planted them around his houses. One of his most successful was Compton Hill House in Farnham, a wooded four-acre site where the fine loam soil was covered with six inches of leaf mould.

Many of his friends had anecdotes about his expertise. Ron Cooper drove him to consult with specialists at Exbury in Hampshire and noticed that he could distinguish different varieties even as seedlings. Alfred Stevens recalled:

> He was a real specialist on rhododendrons, and appeared to know something of every plant that was cultivated. Despite his physical disabilities [bad leg and old age] he cultivated two gardens and when from time to time he visited me he brought along a rare layered rhododendron. He would drag it out of his car, together with his old fork—one prong missing for as long as I can remember—and a worn-down spade, and find the spot in my garden which he thought most suitable, and proceed to dig a hole and plant it, and I would have to arrange for future cultivation to suit his choice of place. Needless to say, his choice was the best, and if results were slow that was due to the poorness of the soil. That done, he returned his tools to the back of his car, which seems to have been his only tool-shed, filled with such implements as his gardens required.

CHAPTER SIX

Falkner and Farnham Town

The greatest achievement of Falkner's life was to oversee the piecemeal reconstruction of Farnham's town centre to make it look more Georgian. Roderick Gradidge described it in 1981 as 'England's Williamsburg', meaning that the town was an extraordinary mix of old buildings with new ones made to look like the old, where 'old' meant mainly, but not always, 18th-century. Falkner was not averse to anything older but believed that big Victorian buildings were out of place, and that 20th-century Modernism would be a disaster. Today most people who live in the town and have opinions on the subject are proud of Falkner's achievement, but a warning note was sounded by Ian Nairn in the Pevsner volume on Surrey 'The replacement of the truly alien Town Hall in the 1930s was the high water mark: today [1962] preservation has become stultification, so there are now streets, as in Chichester, where there are more Neo-Georgian houses than true Georgian ones.'

Civic projects

Falkner loved the town and was proud of its architectural heritage. His ten-page article on Farnham in the 1916 *Architectural Review,* illustrated by his own sketches, remains one of the best descriptions of the town's history and buildings. In 1911, he joined with Dr Edmund Talbot, the new Bishop of Winchester and thus the occupier of Farnham Castle, Charles Borelli, George Sturt and his old tutor W. H. Allen to inaugurate the Farnham Society which has ever since acted as the town's architectural conscience, vigorous in opposing schemes which might threaten its heritage. Richard Dufty, Chairman 1956-60, recalled that 'at a Society AGM Falkner got up and started lambasting me as a "Civil Service clerk" and the Society as a company of purblind retired officers. But my riposte was that at least we had saved the [fine 18th-century] Ranger's House. "Oh yes," he said, "so you have. Well, full marks for that, even if you are a bunch of so-and-so's".' In his will Falkner bequeathed to the Society his house at 24 West Street and his half share in nearby Wickham House.

We have seen that his first architectural commission was the entrance to the Swimming Bath built to celebrate Queen Victoria's Jubilee in 1897. This was an important part of the town centre and next to the Farnham Liberal Club which had been completed in 1895 by Edwin Lutyens; it was one of Lutyens' earliest commissions and the frontage is impeccably Queen Anne-style with good brickwork. The side adjoining the Swimming Bath entrance is less impressive, and outshone by Falkner's carefully detailed (different patterns and textures, different brick types and colours) brickwork under a bold white cornice. This is brickwork which demonstrates that the town has truly 'arrived', having the first public swimming pool for miles around.

In 1900 his drawings for new Urban District Council Offices were shown at the Royal Academy: the style was vaguely Georgian, not too different from the design which in 1903 was built by Paxton Hood Watson in South Street. He was pleased to point out that his drawings, and not those of Paxton Watson, had been exhibited at the Royal Academy—and that his costings would have been more accurate. In 1909 Farnham Urban District Council purchased Gostrey Meadow, a piece of open ground between the town (Union Street) and the River Wey, to preserve it as an open space for civic recreation. Subsequently Falkner helped design the layout as a civic park, with an elegant drinking fountain and a small pavilion (financed by his friend Borelli) which still stand today.

In 1913 he designed the extension to the nearby Art School in South Street where his old master, W. H. Allen, was still the Principal. Very much in the Georgian box style, it is now (like so many other Georgian houses in Farnham) a solicitor's office.

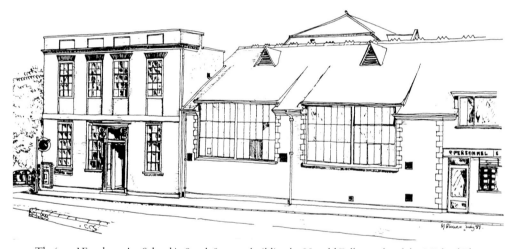

33   The 'new' Farnham Art School in South Street—building by Harold Falkner, sketch by Michael Blower.

Commercial Buildings

In his first decade as an architect Falkner was mainly occupied in designing houses, but he was also architect for two significant commercial projects. In 1904 he designed premises for the Deepcut Dairy Company in Farnborough: a Niven, Wigglesworth and Falkner project illustrated in *The Architectural Review* of 1905. It was really a tea-room with a flat above, built in the Arts and Crafts style with a large Dutch gable in the roof.

34 Doorway at Pilgrim's Motor Works, Farnham.
Sketch by Michael Blower

In the same year, still apparently working for the NWF partnership, he designed premises for the Pilgrim Motor Works in Weydon Lane where the Pilgrim motor car was manufactured 1905-15. This must have been a project which especially appealed to Harold with his love of cars, and *The Farnham Herald* suggested that the town might become 'quite a centre of the motor industry'. Alas, this never happened; the company went bankrupt, though the factory building survived in an altered form (as the Plasmec Works) until 1987 when Michael Blower[1] sketched the elegant neo-Georgian doorways with their carefully constructed brick mouldings and scallop-shells, symbol of the St James pilgrims, under the pediment. These doorways were the sort of feature that a young Falkner might have recycled elsewhere, but, surprisingly, they were swept away when the remains of the factory were finally demolished in 1990.

A third Falkner pre-First World War commercial building was the Electric Theatre, built in 1913 in East Street (near the Royal Deer buildings). Though the name indicated its modernity at the time, it was in fact a cinema rather than a theatre, and its trade was later taken by the Regal Cinema, built nearby in 1933. The Electric Theatre was demolished in 1956, followed some years later by the Regal, and Farnham has been without a cinema since.

The alliance with Charles Borelli

None of Falkner's civic work would have succeeded without his alliance with Charles Ernest Borelli, his life-long friend and ally in the campaign for Farnham's townscape. In his obituary Falkner's old school-friend Alfred Stevens wrote:

Both had keen eyes for everything that was going on in the building line, and if Falkner probably had the main ideas, Borelli was invaluable in helping to carry them out. Falkner alone, with his abrupt manner, would have been able to achieve far less than was done had it not been for Borelli's sociable characteristics, helping him to approach anybody and everybody and crossing the T's and dotting the I's of schemes put forward, not necessarily of their own, but the schemes of anybody who ventured to lift a brick of old Farnham without their blessing.

The Borelli family came from Italy in the 1820s. Two brothers arrived and set up a watch and clock business at 111 West Street, Farnham. They were later joined by four nephews, one of whom, Charles (1843-1917) took over the business which had moved to 36 The Borough. From 1877 it was known as 'Charles Borelli and Sons Watchmakers' and remained in the Borough until it closed in December 1972. The sons were Charles Ernest (1873-1950) and Frank Leonard ['Leo'] (1881-1964). Charles Ernest never married, but his brother Leo (who was also a partner in the family business) was the father of the Catholic priest, Father Charles Vincent Borelli, who lived and worked in Farnham until his death in 1999. The Borelli premises in The Borough, which included barns and gardens behind; have since been sympathetically redeveloped as 'Borelli Yard'. In the process a large number of tiles and other materials stored there by Harold Falkner were unearthed.

Charles Ernest Borelli won a major prize for watch-making in 1894 which resulted in his being made a Freeman of the City of London. He was clearly good at his trade but his main love was the town of Farnham, especially its trees and old buildings. He was elected to the Farnham Urban Council in 1906 and remained a councillor almost without interruption until his death in 1950. Throughout this time he devoted himself to the beautification of Farnham: not only did he have the political skills, enhanced by charm and tenacity; he also was happy, especially since he was a bachelor, to use his considerable personal financial resources to buy and redevelop properties. He had been friends with Falkner, two years his junior, since their time at Farnham Grammar School. Borelli had also attended Farnham Art School, where W.H. Allen had first awakened him to an appreciation of Georgian buildings.[2] They were playing members of Farnham Football Club and Farnham Hockey Club. They were the first joint Secretaries of the new Swimming Baths in 1897. They joined the Royal Flying Corps together in 1918.

Their first joint letter on architectural conservation was published in 1903 in the local newspaper, and was followed by a stream of others over the next 47 years. Theirs was a partnership in which Harold provided the architectural knowledge and Charles the political and financial muscle; neither would have been so effective without the other. From 1911, when Borelli became Chairman of the Urban District Council, until Borelli's death in 1950, little that did not have the approval of Borelli and Falkner got built in Farnham, and much futile destruction of old buildings was prevented.

Borelli was always willing to use his considerable powers of persuasion in the interests of what he considered to be the enhancement of the town's appearance. He always encouraged tree-planting. He had a penchant for Georgian bow-window shop-fronts, and encouraged their construction even where Falkner was not involved. He was utterly opposed to any building of more than three storeys; a principle that was miraculously upheld throughout the 20th century (even when multi-storey car-parks were mooted). He felt strongly that Farnham was a brick town, and talked developers (such as the Regal Cinema directors in 1932) into using brick rather than cement or stucco. These tastes prevailed in Farnham long after his death.

In December 1960 Sir Hugh Casson, leading architect of the 1951 Festival of Britain, spoke to the Farnham Society on *Town Sense*,[3] saying:

> You here in Farnham are living in a beautiful town which has kept its identity and character. That is not due entirely to luck. A great deal of it is due to much hard work and forethought and very often to a few eccentrics—creative nuisances, they might be called. Most towns have them. I hope there are some here. They won't leave things alone. They are an absolute curse to the local authority, but they get their way.

For sixty years Falkner had been such a creative nuisance, and it was Borelli who had backed him. Falkner repaid the compliment in a speech of thanks by recalling that Casson was 'one of the young men who, brought up in the newly formed architectural schools, decided that architecture as practised in the 1920s and 1930s was all wrong and should cease to exist ... [but] now he is suspected of seeing the error of his ways.'

Reconstruction of shops

The first project on which Borelli and Falkner co-operated was a building called *The Goats Head* on the south side of The Borough facing up Castle Street. Only a few doors along from Borelli's shop, it was a public house closed by the magistrates in 1909 on the grounds that Farnham had too many pubs and too much drunkenness. Borelli bought the building and he and Falkner discovered that there was a considerable Tudor building behind the stucco frontage. They stripped back to this and added a staircase and some timber framing from other demolished buildings so that there is now a half-timbered front of *c*.1600 style with a complex pattern of quatrefoils and three oriel windows. Ian Nairn[4] wrote in his usual trenchant style that 'the design corresponds to most of what was there originally, ... but the restored texture is so repellent that the building as a whole seems valueless.' Today the building serves as a shop under the sign of 'The Spinning Wheel' and the comment seems unfair: the building provides an interesting contrast to neighbouring buildings in completely different styles—and disproves the accusation that Falkner and Borelli were only interested in Georgian frontages (which a lesser architect might have opted for in this case).

Borelli had a preference for shops with white Georgian bow-fronted windows. In many cases he persuaded shop-keepers to install or improve them. At 5-7 The Borough (North side), he persuaded new owners to give an originally Georgian building new bow-fronted windows; Falkner was away in the army at the time (1915). After his demobilisation Falkner remodelled the originally Tudor building nearby on the corner with Castle Street (now a travel agent). Sometimes, but not always, Borelli was able to persuade national chain-stores to have shop-fronts in keeping with the local ambience rather than their nation-wide style: after Falkner's successful reconstruction of the *Goats Head/Spinning Wheel*, the next door shop (Sturt's bookshop), 41-42 The Borough was refaced in Tudor style and when it was taken over by Boots *c*.1930 he persuaded them to keep it that way. When the shop on the other side (number 43) came up for redevelopment he persuaded the developer to have a Georgian shop-front.

In 1952 Falkner remodelled the frontage to the Farnham Herald office at 114 West Street, creating a curved bay-window and treating the next-door premises as a classical Georgian private house. The building has a strong white cornice running along below the roof above both premises.

For 104A West Street, next to an elegant Georgian house once owned by Borelli's company, he installed a late-Georgian shop-front brought from London in 1950; there is an identical shop-front, removed from Cornhill, in the Victoria and Albert Museum, and Falkner's might either be from the same shop or a 19th-century copy. The delicate Adam-style moulded decoration around the window contrasts with the tall giraffe-like brick pillars which Falkner, true to his eccentric style, placed in an arcade in front.

35 A sketch (by Michael Blower) of 40 The Borough (16th-century restoration by Falkner) and nos.41-2 (invention by Falkner).

Falkner created, or was influential in the creation of, other Georgian shop-fronts in West Street and The Borough. Where Falkner and Borelli led the way others followed. Aylwin did several, notably at 22 Downing Street (converted from a humble old cottage) and a classical curved front for 22 West Street (now a shop for antique clocks). Both were illustrated in *The Builder.*

At 20A West Street a Georgian bow-fronted shop-front was installed in 1926 by John Kingham, the builder under whom Falkner had trained. In the process a big moulded 17th-century ceiling was uncovered inside. This had been made by a Farnham plasterer in his front room as a half-size trial version of a ceiling for the Earl of Shaftesbury's house in Dorset; it weighs over two tons, being made of five-inch thick plaster over horsehair and is an amazing sight in a small shop. Falkner sketched it but it looks even better today after further restoration work in 1986. Kingham's firm, Tompsett and Kingham, successors to Frank Birch, went on to install a similar shop-front at 84 West Street.

Later in life Falkner told Nigel Temple that the shop-front he was most proud of was the double-fronted premises in East Street for Patrick's Undertakers, which featured plate glass in metal window-frames—a far cry from the neo-Georgian, and subsequently demolished with the general redevelopment of this unfortunate street.

The Falkner-Aylwin Partnership

In Farnham in Falkner's day there was not a lot of competition between architects, though sometimes others came from outside to take key jobs—such as Church House (R.B. Preston, 1909), St Joan of Arc Church (Nicholas and Dixon-Spain, 1930), and schools and churches and county council buildings for which a county architect was used. Lutyens, who had designed the Liberal Club in 1895, moved away soon afterwards to escape from his parents in Thursley. Falkner's competitors were Wonnacott, the Victorian church-builder (architect of the United Reformed Church on South Street), Paxton Watson (who designed the Council Offices, and went on to national fame), H.Y. Margary (who worked near the *Shepherd and Flock* inn at the east end of town), Gilbert and Hodgson of Castle Street, Arthur Stedman, and Guy Maxwell Aylwin.

Of these, Falkner's main rival was Arthur Stedman, like Falkner a self-made architect who was only elected a Fellow of the RIBA later in life. He had been in practice since 1895, and built a pretty classical-style office for himself in South Street (since demolished to make way for Sainsbury's supermarket). He built several houses in the Great Austins area in a vaguely Arts and Crafts style, and many commercial developments—banks, shops, schools. Less talented than Falkner, he was more respected for reliability and for being a safe hand with alterations; appropriately he was appointed Diocesan Surveyor. He arranged for his son Leonard to be properly trained—at the Bartlett School of Architecture to qualify as ARIBA, and five years as pupil of Lutyens (largely spent working on Queen Mary's dolls house)—before joining him as a partner. Their rebuilding of the house at 49 Castle Street is such a perfect Georgian replica that it was mistaken for Falkner. Arthur died in 1958 and in 1964 Leonard was joined by Michael Blower, who subsequently worked on alterations to many Falkner houses such as Tancreds Ford, The Priory and Overdeans Court, and became the leading Farnham architect and architectural historian. The partnership known as Stedman and Blower still continues.

Falkner's most compatible rival was Guy Maxwell Aylwin, like Falkner an old boy of Farnham Grammar School, a former pupil of Niven and Wigglesworth, and a fellow resident of West Street. Aylwin was fourteen years younger, but was much better organised. He had qualified properly at King's College, London, and at the Architectural Association, was a Fellow of the RIBA, had a proper drawing office (the plans for their joint projects were meticulously drawn in colour), and was able to present a respectable face to commercial clients.

In 1927 Falkner joined Aylwin in a partnership. Aylwin provided him with the infrastructure he needed to support his talent, and as part of a drive towards professional respectability he arranged for Falkner to be elected a Fellow of the Royal Institute of British Architects. Falkner liked to say that his membership of RIBA was really against his will. He argued constantly with the Secretary about the subscriptions, and about RIBA's adoption of Modernism:

> 'My objection is the attitude of the Council which led up to … the building of the [RIBA] HQ in Portland Place. I am perfectly aware that the main bulk of the Institute never knew what architecture is, but the leaders of the profession did. Friends of mine Blomfield, Richardson, Maurice Webb, H M Fletcher and some others. They allowed themselves to be bamboozled by a lot of young fools and press agents into the idea that they could shock the public into an interest in building, a procedure that the technical and other press has contrived further to exploit, and they committed in Portland Place the worst example of architectural bad manners'.[5]

In 1939 he resigned, ostensibly over RIBA sponsorship of a Bauhaus exhibition, but continued to call himself 'Late Fellow RIBA by election'.

The Falkner-Aylwin partnership lasted barely three years, though they remained friends for life and Falkner was still using their joint letterhead in 1932. Aylwin was generous in his praise for Falkner a decade later:

> … the *enfant terrible* of Farnham, and one of its most illustrious sons. I have seen him feeling his way through an early 'Voysey' influence to a sound 'Georgian' phase, and later to the 'craft' phase in which he still finds himself, not, I think, yet content with his adventures. In all this has been a touch of greatness which the world has yet to recognise. My two years of rather explosive partnership with him carry few regrets on my part, and the inevitable 'blow-up' has not prevented us remaining good friends and neighbours. We share a mutual respect which in his case is generous, in mine inevitable.[6]

The business was later taken over by his son John Aylwin, who was rather less appreciative of Falkner, perhaps because he got to know him too late in life. After John's death in 1999 the Aylwin architectural business was wound up.

The partnership of Falkner and Aylwin built few houses. One was The Priory (see chapter 3). Another was Knole House, which Falkner designed for W.H.

Allen's successor as Head of Farnham Art School (again, a feature is a large studio); it is now called Falcon House, and its elegant Flemish-bond brickwork still delights those who pass it on the public footpath leading off Old Park Lane. Not far away on Castle Hill is Hill House, again in mellow brick in the neo-Georgian style, built in 1928 for Major-General Sir Edward Perceval who used to live next door at the genuinely early 18th-century brick mansion, The Grange: it was a good imitation, except for the lack of cornice.

They collaborated on the internal adaptation and external re-fronting of Aylwin's 18th-century Wickham House in West Street (illustrated in *Architect and Building News*, 14 August 1931); again, the brickwork is masterly, though the portico over the front door is overpoweringly large.

Apart from the rebuilding of the Town Hall (see below) their partnership was most active in working on pubs. This work, usually commissioned by large breweries, provided a steady source of income at a difficult economic time, and was probably secured by Aylwin rather than Falkner.[7] Farnham has always had an extraordinarily large number of pubs, due originally to the fairs in Castle Street and cattle markets in South Street, and in the 19th century to the hop trade and the soldiery from Aldershot. In 1900 the ratio of pubs to local inhabitants was twice the national average. From time to time the magistrates closed some on the basis that there were simply too many: when they closed the *Goats Head* in 1909 there were 20 pubs within a quarter-mile radius of it.

For Falkner and Aylwin the business was mainly a matter of improving existing pubs. They rebuilt *The Seven Stars* in East Street and *The Jolly Farmer* in Runfold in neo-Tudor style, a style which Englishmen feel the most appropriate for pubs. In a slightly more modern, but still 'traditional', style, they built another

36 *The Seven Stars*, East Street, Farnham. Sketch by Michael Blower.

pub in Runfold, *The Princess Royal*, and rebuilt the *Alliance* on the corner of Downing Street and West Street. The *Alliance*, now an estate agents, has elegant Georgian style windows topped with arches and a chamfered frontage to facilitate traffic visibility. Near the railway station they rebuilt the *Waverley Arms*, and extended the *Railway Hotel* (now called *The Exchange*).

Falkner left his partnership with Aylwin at the end of 1930. As discovered in his earlier partnership with Niven and Wigglesworth, he was not by nature suited to partnership work. He was too opinionated, impatient and independent-minded—qualities which, rather than mellowing, became stronger as he grew older.

After the split, and after his Town Hall work, he only undertook one job within Farnham town. This was the construction of a new row of almshouses for Sampsons, rebuilt at the far end of West Street, just beyond the Victorian sets of Trimmer's Almshouses and McDonald's Almshouses (built by his rival Arthur Stedman and now listed). A steeply pitched roof, oak front doors and leaded casement windows gives them an Arts and Crafts feel, much preferable to the additions built behind after the Second World War.

Town Hall Reconstruction 1930-34

The most important single architectural project in Farnham in the 20th century was the reconstruction of the Town Hall. This was a joint project between Borelli and Falkner and Aylwin. The site is at the heart of the town: at the bottom of Castle Street, where it joins The Borough. For three centuries a Market House building on oak stilts had stood there in the roadway. In 1866 it was demolished (to relieve traffic congestion!) and the nearby corner site was dignified by a much grander Gothic building which combined the function of Town Hall and Corn Exchange, faced in white brick with red dressings around the windows. The sketch shows how grotesque it must have looked though it was acclaimed when it was built, combining with the nearby Knight's Bank building by Norman Shaw to set a Victorian seal on Castle Street. Falkner's father was present at the great opening banquet and 'came home in such a [alcoholic] state that my mother threatened to lock him out.'[8]

Over a period of years Borelli acquired a controlling interest in the Market House Company that controlled the town hall site, and asked Falkner and Aylwin to design a building more in keeping with the mainly Georgian flavour of Castle Street. They brought in a third architect, T.W. Benslyn who had experience in Birmingham; Falkner said this was in order 'to eat the directors' dinners and soften them up', but in fact the directors were parsimonious about dinners and wanted a counterweight to Falkner who was the main architect involved. The result was a neat neo-Georgian building under a steeply pitched roof, surmounted by a clock and (something which has become a feature of many buildings in Farnham since) a white cupola structure.

On top of the cupola Falkner, acting on his own initiative without authority from the Town Hall Company, placed a weather-vane in the form of a six-foot model, in beaten copper over-gilded, of Sir Francis Drake's 'Golden Hind'. The

37 Victorian buildings in Castle Street replaced by Harold Falkner—above: the 1862 Town Hall (sketch by Nigel Temple); right: Knight's Bank by Norman Shaw (sketch by Harold Falkner).

overall effect is disproportionately tall and of no special historical relevance to Farnham, but is nevertheless striking and has been since copied elsewhere in Farnham. Although it makes no difference to the appearance, the designation 'Town Hall' is a misnomer, since the building is not owned by the local council nor was it financed by them; it does not house their offices, and has no space for public meetings.

The best part of the new Town Hall building (see Plate IX) was the arcaded frontage to The Borough; this was originally opposed by the councillors but Falkner got it built when the Inland Revenue, as potential tenants, wanted more space at first-floor level. This arcade, onto which fronts a row of shops, alternates brick pillars with groups of stone pillars with Doric and Corinthian capitals, the variation giving the impression of a building which has grown over a period of time. At the end the arcade runs under a balcony connecting the Town Hall to the old Bailiffs' Hall, where the balcony is now used by a restaurant.

The Bailiffs' Hall (see Plate X) is Falkner's urban masterpiece. The original building dates from Tudor times. When Falkner started work there, it was dilapidated and the frontage had to be cut back by several feet. Having by then dispensed with his partner architects, he sought drawings of it in earlier times. He substantially rebuilt it as it might have been, with gables, carved leaden rain hoppers, and a convincing reconstruction of patterned Tudor brickwork extending into the interior. He added a tile on the front gable with the twin dates of 1566 and 1934. The whole is connected with the Town Hall building, and the arcade runs below with Ionic capitals, but the bricks and tiles used look significantly older than those used for the Town Hall, which does not pretend to be anything other than a modern building. The Town Hall materials are modern, but the design has some similarities with older town halls in Surrey. In particular, the brick arcading below and the cupola and clock above are reminiscent of the old Georgian town halls in Reigate, Haslemere and Godalming (the 'pepper pot').

Nearby, a little way up Castle Street, Norman Shaw had designed in 1867 an overpowering neo-Elizabethan building for the Knight family bank (later taken over by Lloyds Bank). It was twice as tall as any other building in Castle Street, and its half-timbered upper storeys projected over the street (see Fig. 37). Falkner recalled[9] that 'It towered up above the street like a great ship's stern of four storeys: an overhanging mass of oak and medieval detail.' When it was built it was praised for the way in which it outshone the modest brick Georgian buildings of Castle Street, but by 1927 the opinion was that it clashed with them.

At the same time as the new Town Hall was being built Borelli persuaded the Directors of Lloyds Bank to replace it with something less overpowering and more in keeping with the 18th-century flavour of Castle Street. The resulting building, designed by an associate of Guy Dawber, is in brick with an impressive 18th-century cornice and pediment, and blends in well. Falkner himself liked Norman Shaw's building, albeit that it was so out of character with the street as a whole. He admired Norman Shaw, the most renowned architect of his day, and he had trained under Frank Birch, the Farnham builder who had built Knight's Bank. He made careful records of the building, and salvaged the two big chimneys; one he placed over the reconstructed Bailiffs' Hall and the other over the *Bush Hotel* opposite. Towering edifices of fluted brick, they make remarkable architectural landmarks in their new positions.

The *Bush Hotel* was originally a Tudor inn, being remodelled by Falkner and Aylwin with a new entrance for cars. In the process Falkner uncovered a 16th-17th-century wall-painting, at the entrance to the current dining room, which he 'restored' with great enthusiasm.

Paradoxically, both the Norman Shaw bank building and the old Town Hall would have been listed Grade II today, making their demolition impossible. It would be said, with some justification, that they were remarkable Victorian buildings which provide an interesting contrast in a street of mainly Georgian appearance.

Falkner and Farnham Town Planning after 1934

Arguably Falkner's greatest legacy to Farnham was not the buildings he converted or built, but the influence he exerted, usually via Borelli, on the townscape as a whole. But for him many more old buildings would have been unsympathetically redeveloped or pulled down, as happened in the East Street redevelopment which took place just after his death. Although Falkner built nothing in the town after 1934, he continued to live in West Street and took a keen interest in all town developments. He continued to be Borelli's friend and main adviser, and to give his views to all who would listen. He kept up a lively correspondence with *The Farnham Herald* on town planning matters. I quote from his letters to the paper at some length because they portray both his views and his sense of humour.

His main concern was with the overall appearance of the town rather than individual buildings. Despite his strong sympathy for the past, he was not against new developments because they were modern. A keen motorist himself, he did not oppose the controversial bypass road which caused destruction of a cluster of old buildings near Hickley's Corner to the south of the town centre. Up to the age of 87 he continued to write to the press with suggestions for road traffic improvements.

In 1954 the main town planning debate centred on The Hart Ground, a big open space close to the centre of Farnham. Falkner was passionately in favour of keeping it mostly as an open space, surrounded by terraces of flats. In an article for the *Farnham Herald*, 12 November 1954, he wrote:

'The matter of the development of The Hart Ground, casually mentioned in a committee report where we hardly expect to see anything more important than that "the extension to Mrs So-and-So's woodshed is approved" is of immense importance.

'... My advocacy of terraces may seem, to some, surprising. It arises from (1) the enormous cost of roads and services. (2) As everyone (except the privileged classes, miners and dockers) has much the same income, house snobbery has ceased to exist. (3) That much as I respect gardeners, only one out of ten persons has the ability or energy to garden, and the hiring of someone else to do the work is out of the question. (4) The detached villa or bungalow in its own ground is eating up far too much of the country. (5) Only by some such combined effort can anything of architectural dignity be accomplished.

'… The important thing is that the inhabitant and that the powers-that-be, other than the Urban Council, should be aware of what is going on before sanction is given.'

Falkner lost the battle for terraced buildings, but the area is still largely an open space. It is now a car-park serving Safeways supermarket.

In 1963 there was furious debate concerning the redevelopment of East Street at the heart of Farnham. The modernists wanted to sweep away the old shops, several of which (such as the Gas Board showroom) dated back to Tudor times, and replace them with new buildings in the modern idiom. Falkner, allied with Aylwin and many others, thought this would be disastrous. *The Farnham Herald* of 22 March 1963 was full of letters on the subject, among them one from Falkner:

'In my letter written before the publication of the "exciting" drawing, I suggested that the developers might find some difficulty in finding an architect capable of building on this site in accordance with the traditions of the town. Obviously they have.

'In order to realise how this situation has arisen it is necessary to retrace some architectural history. In about 1933 Hitler expelled some architects from Germany who were building in what was called an advanced manner. The real fact was that Germany was immensely poor and they were cutting everything of an architectural tradition from their buildings. This and certain American influences resulted in the spread of these stripped or "functional" buildings.

'In 1931 Howard Robertson [became] Director of the Architectural Association School. He immediately reversed the teaching of the school and said: "Put away all your books, abandon the study of architecture, and do whatever function or structure of steel-framed building suggests."

'The students jumped at this. It meant giving up study of all forms of architecture or proportion or any of those tedious things, and was vigorously supported by all the technical press. Hence there has grown up a species of so-called architects who are capable of inadequately clothing steel-framed buildings and nothing more …

'This movement got a great boost from the 1951 collection of architectural freaks known as The Festival of Britain.…Consequently a new 'school of architects' arose and these … now rule … Hence we now have an architect who, although I believe he is trying to please the inhabitants, produces this "exciting" design.

'He says the character of Castle Street cannot be revived. The fact is that he and his contemporaries do not know how to do it … that this can be done is shown in the new police station and the courts of flats behind Firgrove House.

'There is no need to destroy … a 16th century building … There is a ruthlessness about these proceedings to which a stop ought to be put. The process is to "put a bulldozer through the lot" destroying everything.'

In another letter to *The Herald* he argued 'The higgledy-piggledy development of the area is its greatest charm. It is evidence of the independence of the builders.'

On the assumption that the whole street would indeed be swept away Falkner subsequently suggested (*Farnham Herald*, 29 March 1963) a sweep of new buildings in the style of 18th-century Bath. Although he labelled it 'provisional' and his previous arguments for terraces at The Hart have some validity, it must be said that this design was not very appropriate for Farnham either. The redevelopment would never have happened when Borelli ruled, but he had died in 1950. In his letters to *The Farnham Herald* Falkner urged the public to go and see the Council's plans and make their views known, but he hinted darkly that whatever the people said the authorities would push the plans through. He was right, and perhaps it was as well that he died in November 1963 before the scheme was implemented.

In 1964 all the old shops and other buildings on the north side of East Street were swept away and replaced by brick and concrete blocks of shops with offices and flats above; rising to four storeys with a flat roof. Although it was called The Woolmead it had nothing to do with any wool meadow and was a deliberate contrast to the rest of the town. It soon seemed horribly dated and brutalist, and debate raged over new proposals for its replacement. By 1999 everyone agreed that it should be demolished, the only controversy being over what should replace it. The town planners suggested enlarging the area for redevelopment, threatening the only remaining listed building in the area, Brightwell House, together with its public tennis courts and bowling green. This provoked a storm of criticism that they were thinking of the wishes of commercial developers rather than the townspeople who might prefer existing open spaces and old buildings. The Farnham Society and the Farnham Trust won the battle to retain the Listing of Brightwell House, but once again, as in Falkner's day, there was apprehension at the planners' idea 'to put a bulldozer through the lot' and nervousness that officials' views would prevail regardless of the public's preferences.

The arguments of 1963 were brought out again in 2002 and 2003 regarding further development of the East Street area. On the one hand there were those who argued that Farnham had a special heritage of Georgian buildings of grace and elegance, and nothing should be done to upset this. At the very least, there should, as under the Falkner-Borelli regime, be nothing with a flat roof-line or over three storeys.

On the other hand there were those, including most architects, who argued that to continue to build in the Georgian style would fossilise Farnham as a pastiche theme park. There were already more fake Georgian shop-fronts than real ones: surely new developments should not only make use of contemporary materials but also modern design? It was further argued that there might be an advantage in providing a contrast to existing older buildings—provided, of course, that the new designs were 'high quality' (a description which every architect uses about his own work).

In terms of public appreciation the most successful townscape projects in Farnham over the past thirty years have been the Lion and Lamb Yard shopping centre, an outstanding redevelopment of a central pedestrian enclave in a mix of 17th- and 19th-century styles, and the residential village for the Surrey Institute of Art and Design, which has combined traditional components such as dormer windows and tile-hung upper storeys with a requirement for modern accommodation at budget cost.

But the local council are also swayed by economic considerations, which are in turn affected by lump-sum premia obtainable from supermarkets and (encouraged by new government guidelines) maximising the amount of residential accommodation to be crammed onto the site. In this context there is less room for architectural heritage or for the people of Farnham to continue to play on public tennis courts in the heart of the town. In the final resort it is Waverley Borough Council, rather than just the citizens of Farnham, who will determine the shape of the town.

CHAPTER SEVEN

The Dippenhall Fantasy

From 1920 until he died in 1963 Falkner indulged his architectural fancies by building nine private houses in Dippenhall. They were sited on corners of farmland away from any village centre; they were structurally unsound; they did not comply with building regulations; their internal layout was unsatisfactory; they failed to appeal to buyers. Despite all this, they are works of genius, a brilliant combination of imagination with a love of old buildings, some magical architectural fantasies buried among the woods and fields.

A hundred years earlier Pugin, protagonist of the Gothic Revival, had created one similar grouping near Farnham—a big stone barn, a gatehouse with chambers above the gateway, a farmhouse with a duckpond, a ruined, ivy clad and possibly genuine monastery wall and window. This was an essay in the Picturesque, looking convincingly medieval. Situated on the edge of the Peper Harow estate, Falkner would have passed it every time he went to visit Gertrude Jekyll at Munstead.

Disney create the great fantasy buildings of today, but in Britain between the world wars there was not the wealth around to sustain much architectural fantasy. Falkner's Dippenhall buildings are comparable (albeit less concentrated) with the village which Clough Williams-Ellis created at Portmeirion in North Wales. In both cases the architect was free to indulge his own imagination, free of clients and out of the way of building inspectors. Disneyland and Portmeirion may be criticised for being artificial pastiche. Falkner at Dippenhall was different. His inspiration came from finding bits of old buildings, or even whole buildings, and re-assembling them to form a new building looking like an old one.

In his lifetime the Dippenhall houses were seen as the work of a man with a confused mind at the edge of reason and steadily becoming more eccentric. A *Country Life* architectural critic was told by his editor that they were not serious architecture and therefore not worth writing about. In 1968, five years after Falkner's death, an article by Nicholas Taylor on the Dippenhall houses was published in *The Architectural Review* which made the architectural world take Falkner seriously. Phrases such as 'architectural super-tramp', 'inspired lunacy', 'the romantic decay of an Edgar Allen Poe filmset', 'gravity-defying gables' set the tone; but 'the topsy-turviness seems not just accident but perversely intended accident ("action architecture")'. Taylor noted that at least three of the houses,

38 Falkner's drawing of a gable at Castle Cary
(a possible model for Burles in Dippenhall).

Meads, Halfway House and Burles, were derelict at the time, but still praised Falkner's original genius as 'the physical embodiment of the dreams of a king of perspectivists: the crooked lines, the hairy textures, the paradoxes of scale. At a time of paper architecture, when the applause of an Academy private view mattered more than the actual performance on a Surrey hillside, only Falkner had the perverse integrity actually to build his perspectives.'

Architectural Salvage

Falkner's Dippenhall buildings represent a triumph of architectural salvage. This was not, of course, a new activity—Rome had been a source of material for centuries, so had the English monasteries since their Dissolution, and antiquaries such as Horace Walpole and Sir John Soane had delighted in finding ancient artefacts to incorporate in their buildings—but Falkner sought out more mundane objects such as floors and beams. Today architectural salvage is big business: old doors, windows, fireplaces and timbers which would have been thrown away fifty years ago are now lovingly recycled. In Falkner's day this was rare; they were usually burnt or left to rot. He was a re-cycler before his time, a man with a magpie's eye for interesting bits of old buildings and an artistic genius for incorporating them in newer buildings.

When he was young major sources were the ship-breaking yards in Devon and Portsmouth, which yielded magnificent timbers for floors and beams, and old barns in general. The twenty years following World War II were a golden era for seekers of old material. Many buildings, especially in London, were suffering from war damage, or from decay following years in which maintenance was impossible. Great country houses had become a total anachronism: in 1955 they were being demolished at the rate of two every week. Farmers were discovering that big new steel-framed barns, for which no planning permission was required, were much more efficient than old wooden ones. In the towns the Modern Movement was preaching that old buildings should be demolished to make way for modern architecture.

Falkner toured Southern England searching for material, relying on others to drive as he got older. He set up a storage point at Dippenhall in one of the sheds of the Dippenhall Lime Works in Crondall Lane. By a happy co-incidence the Works were taken over, during his lifetime, by his tenant David Gillespie who manufactured plastic materials for stage sets (very useful when he came to own a Falkner house); subsequently the Works were used by another Falkner house-owner, Fred Warrren, for the manufacture of 18th-century style panelling.

The Dippenhall Land

Dippenhall is an area of fertile farmland two miles west of Farnham. The Falkner family had owned land here since 1750, and lived in Dippenhall House which was only demolished in 2002. Harold's father and grandfather had farmed the land, and so did his elder brother when he came of age. Harold, who had been born after his father died, inherited no Dippenhall land, but bought some later on his own initiative in order to build houses.

He must have hoped that by building in a rural area out of town he might escape the building inspectors. Even as a young man he had been disinclined to spend effort on building regulations, the artistic detailing and overall effect being much more important in his eyes, but his houses had been structurally sound. During his lifetime building regulations had become more comprehensive and more rigorous. As he got older he became increasingly impatient in his attitudes to them. In the end they caught up with him and when he died his final Dippenhall building, The Black Barn, was the subject of a prosecution by the building inspectors.

There was no office work for Dippenhall. He drew no detailed architectural plans. He pieced together each house over a period of years, according to when he picked up components and had the time to install them. Even during his partnership with Aylwin he kept Dippenhall as his private world, outside the partnership. Aylwin later commented: 'What he was doing was building—the thing he always wanted to do. He cut out all the things he hated: drawing, office work, documentation, very nearly the Public Health Act and its officers, and—most of all—clients.'

The Builders

His instructions to builders had never been precise. He preferred to use builders he could trust and then let them get on with the work using their initiative. For many of his Great Austins buildings he had used a local builder called Mills who recalled that Falkner gave him sketches and instructions scribbled on the back of old envelopes which he had to interpret as best he could.[1] At Dippenhall he even dispensed with a building contractor. At first he employed just three workers—Alfred Hack, his brother Bert Hack, and a joiner, Algie Vass. After some years just the loyal Alfred Hack and a friend, Hugh Pearlman, remained, plus occasional gypsies and vagrants.

The only experienced craftsman was Falkner himself. He had always been more interested in the craftwork than the overall planning, and now he could allow his imagination and carving skills full scope. He was never happier than when up a ladder, or laying bricks, or carving wood and stone. One might view this as the sheer idiosyncrasy of an old man, but when Falkner started his work at Dippenhall he was still in his 40s and far from his dotage. Michael Drury has suggested[2] that in fact he was pursuing Ruskin's ideal of the medieval master builder who worked on the building with his bare hands as sculptor and mason as well as designer. William Morris had espoused this ideal, and abandoned his ambition to become an architect after his apprenticeship in the office of G.E. Street because buildings had to be created at second-hand (i.e. via a builder) and there was not enough scope for the individual craftsmanship advocated by Ruskin. Only a few Arts and Crafts architects, among them the young Detmar Blow who had acted as assistant to Ruskin, made a wholehearted attempt to achieve this.

Thus every one of his houses at Dippenhall has an original and individual touch, displayed both in the overall design and in the touches of craftsmanship in carvings, stonework and panelling. As Falkner got older the originality remained but the structural quality, which was excellent when he was younger, steadily deteriorated. The houses carried seeds of their own destruction: poor foundations, no proper damp-course, faulty breeze blocks, badly laid bricks, death watch beetle in the old timbers, inadequately supported beams, haphazard electric cabling, roofs and walls which let in water.

Dean's Farm houses (Dippenhall Grange, Deans Knowe, The Barn, Overdeans Court), 1922-1930

In an interview with the *Farnham Herald* for 29 August 1980 his niece, Beryl Falkner recalled:

> In 1920 the Trimmer family, who lost their only son in the war [and had given the land for the Farnham Swimming Baths in 1897], sold their estate. Falkner bought Deans Farm—90 odd acres with two houses, seven cottages, and numerous farm buildings at Dippenhall.
>
> My late father farmed the land, HF demolished some of the buildings, took down a barn and stables, and re-erected them in Kiln Field, now a house called The Barn, knocking a hole in another barn to make the archway entrance and a cottage.
>
> He altered the Bailiff's house, Deans, inside and out and converted the farmyard on the south side into a garden. The pond was already there; it collected the rainwater from the farm buildings. He altered The Grange inside and out, adding a new drawing room, and enlarged the garden. It is not a Tudor cottage converted, as sometimes stated, but is reputed to have been built some time in the 1800s.
>
> In 1925 he bought another barn from the new owner of Runwick House and had nowhere to put it, so he bought a corner of land from my late father. All the timbers were marked, numbered and re-erected with the curve they had on the wall at Runwick. The filling-in stone came from the old Deans farm buildings and he himself did the carving of the stone on the hall window. The house was called Haberdeans after the field. The first occupant did not like the name and called it Hardwick Hall. The third occupant re-christened it Overdeans Court, by which name it is still known.

All four of these houses are now Listed Grade II. The main farmhouse, called The Grange, was originally early 18th-century and had been enlarged c.1800, but was still very much a farmhouse surrounded by barns, granary and piggeries. Falkner transformed it into an 18th-century country house by adding a large panelled drawing room with bedrooms above and refacing the extended south front, with its newly symmetrical range of sash windows, in 18th-century brick below a roof parapet. He embellished the interior with panelling salvaged from elsewhere and by bringing in a black and white marble floor for the hall (taken from the demolished Grosvenor House in London, and since removed). He replaced the main entrance door by a Georgian one with a deep shell hood carved with a pelican pecking its breast to feed its young, reputedly salvaged by him from London—or did he carve it himself, one never quite knows with Falkner? Either way the heavy hood had to be replaced later with a locally made fibreglass copy as it was not well enough fixed to Falkner's new south front wall. The garden was enlarged with terraces and a lily pond. Having transformed the old farmhouse into a gentleman's residence he renamed it more stylishly as 'Dippenhall Grange'.

He also enlarged the nearby timber-framed cottage, which had been used by the bailiff, by adding a second storey with weather-board cladding and a gabled brick porch: this house was renamed 'Dean's Knowe'.

He drove a hole through another brick cottage, which now makes an attractive gatehouse with a high beamed arch, to his next house, The Barn, a half-timbered building combining Arts and Crafts style with old components. The central portion comprises five wooden bays of an old barn, flanked by the addition of a

39 Entrance front of The Barn, Dippenhall.

stone bay on each side. The massive roof comes almost to the ground on the entrance front. Inside there is a tall great hall with a central chimney supporting a beamed roof which has held up against the winds surprisingly well. On each side of the hall is a staircase and a long beamed corridor taking up the north aspect. Off this corridor open the principal rooms, one with panelled doors salvaged from elsewhere, and another with a low plaster ceiling (said to have come from an old house in Kent) supported by an evil-looking wooden pillar reputed to have come from between the decks of a ship. It has wide walnut floorboards. Everywhere the massive beams are supported by carved brackets, clearly old but too finely worked to have come from the original barn. The south-facing garden has a formal layout with pergola, two narrow lily ponds with a well-pond between, and flanking gazebos. It is typical of Falkner's adaptation of Gertrude Jekyll.

At one time Pat Muszynski was Falkner's tenant at The Barn. He told her that the door to the dining room had come from Hampton Court. She remembers him affectionately: 'He was not anti-woman, he was very kind to me (living on my own with three young children). He was bluff, but polite and helpful. We always thought of him as an impressionist architect because his buildings looked wonderful but were very badly finished.' At the time the south-west wing of the house was rented by the artist Tom Luzny, who found the great hall ideal as a studio for huge paintings in the style of his master, Frank Brangwyn. After Falkner's death The Barn became derelict, once the setting for a big 'acid-house' party—for which its isolation and weird atmosphere must have made it very suitable. Subsequently it was immaculately restored by new owners.

Overdeans Court is the longest and craziest of the Dippenhall houses. Each end is composed of an old barn which Falkner moved to the site, and the portion in between, which is set at a slight angle to the barns so that the overall shape is a shallow 'C', incorporates an old cowshed and some modern infilling disguised to look old including a stone window with gothic trefoil tracery—carved by Falkner

40 Window at Overdeans Court, Dippenhall, salvaged or carved by Falkner. Note the irregular tracery.

or salvaged by him from an old church. The exterior is a timber-framed structure, the panels between the timbers originally filled with brick in a herringbone pattern but since replaced with white plaster. The huge roof used old tiles which have had to be replaced, as has the exterior plaster which allowed damp to penetrate. An overhang on the southern side provides a garden loggia, which is now a kitchen extension..

Inside there are typical Falkner idiosyncrasies. In the drawing room, composed of the bigger barn, is a minstrels' gallery with awkward access and a tall mullioned window where the only opening part requires a ladder to

41 Entrance front of Overdeans Court, Dippenhall.

use it. There is a salvaged Jacobean ceiling in a small room, and carvings by Falkner on the ends of the staircase balusters. As with all the Dippenhall houses, successive owners have had to spend huge amounts putting right Falkner's structural errors, but have done so willingly to preserve a unique environment. Over the years the building has been altered many times, but now that it has been listed Grade II the structural work requires special expertise and the most recent changes have been designed by the Falkner experts Roderick Gradidge and Michael Blower.

Meads, Halfway House and Old Timbers, Dora's Green Lane, 1930-36

Beryl Falkner recalled: 'He next bought a barn from Will Hall, Alton, and again had nowhere to put it but was not allowed to buy any more of father's Dippenhall land. However, nothing could stop him—he would have his own way—and he erected Meads on [our] Dippenhall land. Next came Halfway House from left-over bits and pieces.' For many years after these houses were built Falkner was obliged to let them (or lend them to relatives) rather than sell them. One might think that this was because of the recession or their poor construction, but in fact, as Beryl hints, there were also problems with the land title. They were made even more unsaleable by Falkner's neglect of basic maintenance, and at the time of his death were in danger of becoming ruins.

Meads (originally called Baldridges) is now Grade II Listed. This is the house where Falkner is said to have left a tree growing inside. It is really just two old barns joined together. The eventual owners spent 25 years putting the structure in good order—but they did so willingly because they thought the house was such a visual joy.

Halfway House is a cottage-style house, with two gabled dormer windows, rendered walls and casement windows in stained wooden frames. It is joined onto Old Timbers which is in the same style, with timber frame and gables projecting from a barn-like roof. Both houses have a wealth of exposed timber inside, substantiating the fact that they originated from old barns. In the 1990s the owner of Old Timbers knocked down a garden wall and found it had no foundations. He then discovered that the house was held together by a big timber joist which had almost completely rotted away after 50 years. Despite all this, he and his family love the house.

Burles and Burles Lodge, off Crondall Lane, 1937-63

Falkner worked for a long time on these two houses, which in many respects were incomplete at his death. The workmanship became increasingly slipshod although he retained his talent for building a film-set. The site is on a slope opposite an old clunch or chalk quarry. He had to start by terracing the slope, and used the stones he dug up to make foundations for the houses and the eccentric Folly in the garden. He mixed the stones with cement, and for the floors and other internal surfaces brought in breeze material from the local Gas Board. He made his own breeze blocks on site, confounding the suspicions of the building inspectors by demonstrating that they were stronger than their testing machine. He brought in old timbers and old bricks, but there were no proper beam-ties, the walls were poorly joined together and badly pointed and the front wall started to come away from the others.

Burles is two barns from Gloucestershire, with an old granary at one end standing partly on staddle-stones (see Plate XII). It is, of course, normal for an old granary to stand on staddle stones to keep out rats—but these are incongruously incorporated into the wall at a height of five feet. The barns have been assembled with a long projecting upper floor on the south side which Falkner claimed to be the longest overhang in England and *The Architectural Review* described as 'a kind of half-timbered millipede'. On the north side there is a medley of special effects, with small gables, a jutting bathroom window, a drainpipe incongruously dated 1857, and brick buttresses giving the appearance of a moated grange. Falkner added an assortment of items salvaged from elsewhere, including a medieval lead water tank, and gilded internal double doors said to be from a Venetian gondola. These items have now disappeared, but the house is still full of ancient ceiling timbers and has some fine old carving notably over the main fireplaces. The dining room is spectacular—fully panelled walls, wide old floor boards which Falkner said he had obtained from a ship-breaker, and a magnificent Jacobean wooden chimney-piece carved with dragons, cherubs and Ionic pillars. This alone justifies the house being Listed Grade II.

Burles Lodge was unfinished when he died, though it was subsequently tenanted. The main floor windows and doors are in 18th-century style, though there is no attempt at symmetry and the bedroom floor is a jumble of small cottage-style rooms with sloping ceilings and exposed timbers. Since becoming owners in 1975 the Warrens have had to rebuild much of it. Fortunately they could see the potential, as well as the problems, and their professional business was making replicas of 18th-century woodwork. Thus, apart from the major structural work, they have repaired the internal panelling (the main reception rooms were designed to fit old panelling which Falkner had brought in), some of the carved fanlights and display cabinets (others were past repair), and refixed to the walls the elaborate 18th-century door surrounds. The panelled dining room, the most fully Georgian room in the house, has some Grinling Gibbons-type carvings, a plaster carved ceiling with a tondo in the centre, and the owners have hung a portrait of Harold Falkner by John Verney over the mantel. The front door has a particularly impressive portico and pediment salvaged from somewhere but it is difficult to access from the drive as it is up one floor without an obvious external stairway.

Even odder is the garden 'folly' on two floors. Built into the side of the hill, the lower level has an open side with Ionic pillars supporting a classical pediment, said to have been salvaged from a blitzed house in London; it provides a suitable niche for a classical statue. The upper level, which is accessed from the higher

42 Garden folly at Burles, Dippenhall.

garden of Burles next door, looks more like a Georgian gazebo; it has sash windows on three sides and is built of brick with a curved tiled roof. Today the whole is covered with ivy which makes it look even more picturesque. One might think that the ivy will destroy it but the owners believe it is the only thing that prevents it falling down.

True to Falkner's sense of theatre, the two houses would make a splendid film-set, enhanced by the way he made use of the slope to provide terraces and pools and caverns.

Grovers Farm and The Old Barn, Runwick Lane, 1958-63

In July 1958, Harold Falkner bought Grovers Farm, comprising 37 acres, an almost derelict house and two cottages. He altered the house by tearing out the inside, incorporating an old granary or oast house, and putting on a new front. The result is pure theatre, visually dramatic and structurally inadequate. The new front was very much in the Georgian style: four bays of sash windows with 12 panes on the ground floor and nine panes above; an elaborate front door (said to have been salvaged from Lloyds Bank in Farnham), with Corinthian pillars and scallop entablature and a circular window to one side (see Plate XIII); along three of the four sides he built a parapet with big white cornice with modillon-bracketed eaves. To the rear there is no parapet or cornice, and Falkner's roofs include in one corner a timber overhang in the Tudor style. The overall effect is rather overpowering for a farmhouse right on the road, and it is not true to the historical core of the house. But it is grandly theatrical.

Inside he installed a large oak staircase said to have been brought from Itchel Manor, a burned-down house near Crondall. There is also a profusion of wood panelling and old timbers, so that the overall effect is of a house which has developed over the centuries—as indeed it had, albeit not quite in the way that a casual visitor might think.

Fortunately the house was taken over by successive owners who recognised both its artistic potential and its structural faults. David and Ann Gillespie, who knew and liked Falkner, bought the house from his estate and finished it off in appropriate manner. As former theatre designers, who set up a plastic mouldings business in Dippenhall, they were ideally suited for this. They put in fake 17th-century ceilings and real old wooden internal pediments, salvaged from old buildings as Falkner would have done, and built new garden walls of local clunch stone inset with classical bas-reliefs (see Plate XIV). The next owners brought in more panelling, and a salvaged stained glass piece in the hall window. They prevented total collapse of the house by renewing the main fireplace where some broken bricks supported the main ceiling beam and a leaky chimney was a smoke and fire hazard, and by replacing a tree trunk, which Falkner had used to hold up the bedroom floor when he removed a wall, with a steel support disguised as a classical pillar. Falkner's poor drainage and amateurish underfloor electric heating was removed, the poorly laid brickwork was repointed and the gaps around the windows were sealed. Now the house is at last structurally sound, and even more interesting than Falkner left it.

In February 1963 Falkner's application to build 16 new houses on the adjacent farmland was rejected. The land remains farmland still.

The Old Barn (originally called Black Barn), the conversion of a 150-year-old barn which was unfinished at Falkner's death, had a sad history. Falkner was greatly upset when Alfred Hack, his last faithful workman and 90 years old at the time, fell from the roof to his death.

Subsequently Falkner was prosecuted for failing to observe building regulations, in particular the bye-laws concerning foundations, load-carrying structures, and damp-proof courses in cavity walls. His solicitor, Michael Garrood, recalled:[3]

> Harold refused to plead guilty because he had written the original regulations for Farnham Council in the 1920s and knew them better than anyone; unfortunately he was unaware that they had been revised many times before 1960!
>
> The trial took place on a hot summer's day before Farnham magistrates chaired by Mr Bertie Dymott J.P., who I thought was rather pompous. As the hearing progressed it got hotter and hotter and Harold suddenly interrupted the proceedings, standing up and saying to Mr Dymott, 'Young man, may I take my jacket off?' Mr Dymott with a twinkle of amusement in his eye just said, 'Certainly, Mr Falkner' and, taking off his jacket, Harold revealed both belt and braces holding up his shabby trousers.
>
> He was convicted of several offences and fined but refused to accept the decision and we appealed all the way to the Court of Appeal. Some of his convictions stood and we were given leave to appeal to the House of Lords on a point of law. Unfortunately Harold died before the hearing could take place, and his Executors abandoned the Appeal.

After his death the barn was rebuilt, though Falkner's idea of a big brick gable survived, with a connected building, Runwick Hill, and using old bricks and timbers as Falkner would have done.

The Anecdotes

There are many anecdotes about Falkner, and, since he became increasingly eccentric as he got older, it is likely that most of them are true. This is especially likely in relation to his Dippenhall years. The purchaser of one house complained that the garage doors opened inward. Falkner responded by suggesting that a hole should be knocked in the back so that the car could be driven through, the doors closed, and the car backed into place. In another house the gable facilitated water leaking into the interior: Falkner dealt with this by installing an indoor gutter so that the water could be carried away. At Meads the complaint was that the cracks in the wall were so large that a mouse could jump through; Falkner suggested that the time to get worried was when the cracks became so large the cat could jump through too.

He employed vagrants and gypsies to work on the houses and was unable to supervise them properly. It was rumoured that they cheated him by stealing materials and by undoing overnight the work they had done the previous day.

Wanting the houses to look old, he not only used old bricks and timbers, but went out of his way to make modern materials look old—kicking bricks, deliberately pointing them badly, doing internal work with rusty nails and very rough plaster, getting his men to walk up and down new staircases in their heaviest boots. When using old pine panelling, which was often painted in the 18th century, he liked to strip the paint off and then darken the wood with a weird mixture of old engine oil and other substances.

The Last Falkners at Dippenhall

Harold's elder brother, Charles Frank, took over the family farm at Dippenhall on reaching the age of 21. He had two children, Beryl (1901-88) and Charles Harold (1903-47), who had many happy memories of Uncle Harold coming over for tea at Dippenhall House: he brought them boxes of sweets and loved to play with their toys and their dog.

On becoming an adult, Charles Harold opted for a career in farming but, rather than stay at home to work under his father, he moved away to become a trainee farmer elsewhere. Because of this, or a row with his father, or disapproval of his marriage in 1942 to Gwyneth Edwards, a family rift developed and the family farm at Dippenhall was bequeathed entirely to Beryl. She never married and on her death in 1988 left it to her farm manager, whose grand-daughter had been named Beryl after her. Thus the Falkner family connection with Dippenhall was ended after over two centuries. The family home, Dippenhall House, was demolished in 2002 and has been rebuilt as a Georgian style mansion for a banker.

Harold's nephew Charles Harold died in 1947 while his children, Hugh (born 1943) and Diana (born 1946) were still infants. Harold was kind and caring towards the widowed Gwyneth Falkner and her boy and girl. He arranged for them all to live in his houses at Dippenhall in 1947-52, first at Overdeans Court and then Meads. He paid for his great-nephew Hugh's education at boarding school—first a prep school and then Radley—and was very proud when Hugh excelled at cricket, and very concerned when he got ill—Falkner men tended to die early, and Harold was determined that the family name should continue.

Harold was protective when his nephew's widow re-married, insisting on checking personally whether the new man, Ron Cooper, a naval man turned forester, would be good enough for her. Fortunately it worked out well and they all continued to live happily in Dippenhall. Ron Cooper became a friend, and often drove Harold, who was a notoriously bad driver, on trips to notable gardens and country houses, as far afield as Cornwall and York. While they lived at Dippenhall Harold would join them there for Sunday lunch.

When Hugh was 11 Harold took him, together with his stepfather, on a week-long tour of great houses and cathedrals, dazzling them with his knowledge of architecture and furniture and carving—and amusing them with his eccentricities. Such is the nature of childhood memory that Hugh's most vivid recollection is not of architectural history but of Uncle Harold getting out his pen-knife to cut up the meat on his plate in a restaurant.

Harold tried to make up for the fact that the family farm had been left to Beryl by bequeathing his own Dippenhall properties (Overdeans, Meads, Halfway House, The Barn, Burles and some farmland) to Charles' children, Hugh and Diana. Favouring the Falkner name, two thirds of the proceeds were to go to Hugh and one third to Diana (who was required to change her married name back to Falkner if Hugh died and she inherited the whole).

CHAPTER EIGHT

Artist, Craftsman, Town Planner, Historian

Although Falkner worked almost entirely as an architect in the Farnham area, this was far from a narrow fixation. He sketched widely and skilfully, he had a strong interest in history and town planning—and his work in these fields was widely published in the architectural press: this press was highly professional, and would have published nothing, either as articles or as illustrations, unless it was of quality. Nationally he kept up a lively correspondence and entered for many competitions.

Far from being just an architect of middle-class houses, he excelled as an artist, a craftsman, an architectural historian, and a journalist—and he had plenty of ideas on other subjects from rhododendrons to town planning.

As Artist

Farnham Museum has a big collection of Falkner drawings, which demonstrate his remarkable range and depth of talent. Some are water-colours or pen and ink, but the vast majority are pencil drawings. The illustrations in this book are

43 Falkner sketch.

44 Local sketches by Harold Falkner. Left: Tilford oak; below: barn at Froyle; bottom: Tilford Bridge.

evidence of his talent, albeit that the pen and ink drawings reproduce better than the pencil sketches. As remarked in *The Architectural Review* of October 1918 (accompanying his article on Bradford-on-Avon): 'No method of mechanical reproduction could do full justice to his exquisite drawings in pencil. The half-tone process has its limitations as well as its merits; and indeed it may be safely asserted that no printing method can ever reproduce satisfactorily the soft and varied effects of delicate pencilling.'

In September 1901 *The Artist* magazine published an 11-page article about the young Falkner by G.C. Williamson, praising him as an artist of exceptional talent. The theme of the article, which was much longer than any other that year, was that 'the true architect must first be an artist, and his training ... must be based on his artistic genius.' The article is illustrated by only one architectural plan but many sketches of birds and fishes and gardens, together with his designs for a key

45 Early Falkner drawings in *The Artist*, 1901.

and an illuminated address (in connection with the Swimming Bath project). It described him as

> one of the clever students whom Mr Blomfield has trained, but his special genius in drawing needed but little training. ... His fellow townsmen are beginning to find that they have in their midst an artist who will make a great mark ... and they are using his presence to help in beautifying their town. ... This young man has a future before him, and Farnham may be proud of her son and of his clever and diversified work, all of which bears the hall-mark of genius, tempered by careful thought and attuned to the needs of the occasion, never lacking in the poetry of true beauty.

For a young architect this was high praise, and gratifying publicity.

His early sketches were influenced by Aubrey Beardsley and Art Nouveau, but later his subjects became more architectural—buildings and street scenes, not only

46 Falkner's 1902 drawings of Lombard Street signs.

47 Guildford High Street. Sketch by Harold Falkner.

48 The Town Hall (Pepper Pot) Godalming. Sketch by Harold Falkner.

49 Falkner's sketch of Boston Stump.

50 Falkner's drawing of an old house in Lyme Regis, 1908.

51 A Falkner drawing of Old Totnes.

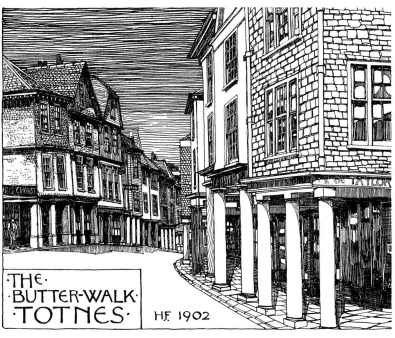

52 Falkner's sketch of Ely Cathedral.

in Farnham but also in other historic towns. His first sketches in *The Architectural Review* were of his first house, Strangers Corner, and were followed in 1903 by sketches of street signs in Lombard Street in London. In the 1920s *The Architects' Journal* frequently published his sketches of old buildings in Oxford, Winchester, Godalming, Guildford, and Wells. Often Falkner's sketch formed their frontispiece, which says much for the quality of his drawing.

Apart from the published sketches, the Farnham Museum collection of Falkner drawings (presented by Sir John Verney who helped save them from being thrown away in 1966) demonstrates his wide range of interests: porches and doorways, china, and furniture, trees, vases, capitals, tablets and tombs. Most are in pencil or pen-and-ink, but there are also some watercolours.

There has always been a strong link between success as an architect and skill in drawing, certainly before the invention of the camera, and even for fifty or sixty years later. Originally this might have been because drawing was the best way to attract and then convince clients, but there is a deeper significance too in that drawing can bring out the essence of a building much better than plans or, in modern times, photographs or computer-aided designs. Despite his artistic skills Falkner was a poor architectural draughtsman. Though he had trained as a builder and as an architect the use of the drawing board and T-square was not something he enjoyed.

As a Craftsman

Falkner liked nothing better than hands-on work as a carver of wood or stone. This goes back to his time as a pupil under W.H. Allen, imbibing the teachings of Ruskin and Morris, and his discovery that he himself had real talent in this field. Thus he personally carved many door-frames and chimney pieces, with a facility for doing this in the styles of previous centuries. He was involved with the stained glass memorial window to his mother who died in 1897. Situated in the south transept of St Andrew's church in Farnham, it is very much in the arts and crafts style.

53 Falkner's drawings of Georgian doorways.

HIGH·WYCOMBE· BUCKS·

UXBRIDGE

9 GROSVNOR RD

Queen Annes Gate.

In the tradition of the Arts and Crafts movement, he liked to design his own door plates and window-catches. But he did not indulge in the custom, cherished by architects then as now, of designing furniture for his houses. His love of carving disproves the accusation that he was a just a facadist architect. Certainly he was concerned with the outward appearance of his buildings, often putting windows where they best suited the facade rather than the internal arrangements, but he took care to embellish interiors with carved stone and panelling, newel posts and friezes. In every house that he built there is somewhere his signature in the form of an individual piece of craftwork made or adapted by him personally.

His obsession with craftsmanship extended to his basic building blocks—his bricks. All architects exercise great care in their choice of bricks, but few take the hands-on approach which Falkner took. He often selected and cut and rubbed each brick himself for maximum effect. Nigel Temple remembers him even in his 80s cutting bricks with two hacksaw blades (ex Barnet and Small's garage where his car was often left) bolted together through their ends and used rather like a spoke shave.

This had the effect of making ordinary brick walls look interesting, as with his very first work, the entrance to the Swimming Baths, built in 1897 and lovingly preserved today. It was especially important in Farnham, where some of the brickwork, such as that of the 1475 Tower at the Castle and the 18th-century Willmer House, is among the finest in the country. At the heart of Farnham is Falkner's reconstruction of the Bailiffs' Hall, his greatest masterpiece in brick, bearing the twin dates of 1566 and 1934, described enthusiastically by Ian Nairn in the Pevsner *Surrey* as 'a creative reconstruction … a brilliant bit of expertise, far better than his Neo-Georgian, giving a delightful composition of niches and shaped gables.'

Cities and Town Planning

Falkner's views on town planning were not confined to Farnham. In his articles on other historic towns he had strong opinions. He was particularly incensed by the tendency to tear down old buildings in the interests of 'progress'. In his writing for the architectural press he was scathing about 'bright young men', particularly if they had the idea that Georgian streets, as in Bath, represented 'a dull monotony'. His comment on the demolition of Robert Adam's elegant 18th-century London Adelphi is typical:

> 'This is not a case of preserving … any sort of archaic structure, but an exceedingly restrained and sober building by one of our most universally accepted architects. … It has been said that the buildings have been marred by Victorian alterations; these are not particularly conspicuous and have been absorbed into the general "mellowness" … The argument about "necessity" is totally wrong … [only] a certain amount of office and shop accommodation is required in this neighbourhood.'

Some might dismiss such comments as the rantings of an old fogey, but Falkner was much more than that in his approach to town planning.

The first cars arrived when he was a young man, and his whole life saw the relentless growth in their numbers. Although he may have seemed a traditionalist, he loved cars and drove all his adult life. He was tireless in drawing up new road schemes to relieve traffic congestion in Farnham, and his proposals for traffic in Oxford and London were published in the architectural press.

He was not against new buildings *per se*, but only when he believed they were 'out of place'. He described the new Battersea Power Station as 'a mistaken effort to give an engineering problem an architectural trimming—as well put lace around a prize-fighter's shorts.'[1]

Although he operated entirely in or near Farnham, where almost nothing was built of more than three storeys, he readily perceived the advantages of high-rise blocks in cities. *The Builder* of 14 January 1927 featured an article by him

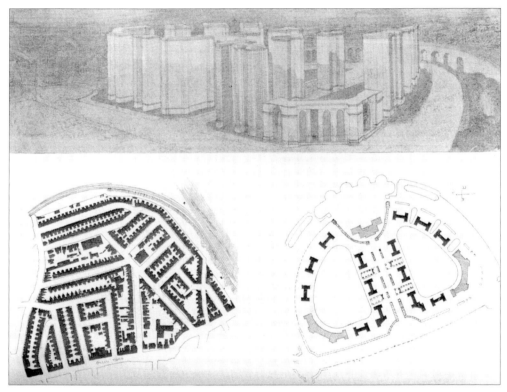

54 A re-housing suggestion for part of Battersea, showing existing layout on the left, and redesigned area on the right. This drawing by Falkner appeared in *The Builder*, 14 January 1927.

proposing the redevelopment of part of Battersea to re-house people in 22-storey blocks of flats. His reasoning could be mid-20th century: more efficient use of land (the land freed up being used for recreation), improved health and sanitation and smoke control, development by the County Council rather than private landlords, and extra cost minimised by using ferro-concrete. He even rehearsed the social requirements: lifts big enough for perambulators, lower floors for shops and clubs, and top floors for laundry. None of this was totally new—Le Corbusier's revolutionary *Vers Une Architecture* had been published in France in 1923 though it did not appear in English until after Falkner's article—but the article does demonstrate that Falkner could see the advantages of a Modernist approach in cities.

In a letter to *The Architects' Journal* of 18 April 1935 he was scathing about the timidity of five-storey urban blocks, their need for lifts and the disproportionate amount of ground. 'If development is to be urban why not go the whole hog and build twenty-storey flats?' and 'shops on the corridors would brighten them up as they have the stations on the Underground.'² Le Corbusier would have supported Falkner's reasoning, and Falkner might well have approved of the Corbusier-style high-rise blocks erected on the Alton Estate in Roehampton in 1956.

National Competitions

Falkner took part in several national architectural competitions and did quite well. For someone without the support of a drawing office, to undertake this work was remarkable. Apart from competing at the Royal Academy and an early competition for cottages, the subjects were all very different from his normal field of individual middle-class houses. At the age of only 24, his designs were chosen for hanging in the Royal Academy: his first building, Strangers Corner, and his Designs for Council Offices in a small Country Town. In the next few years several of his designs were chosen for exhibition at the Royal Academy.

In a 1912 competition for a new town on Lord Aberconway's land in Prestatyn, North Wales, he was placed second (*The Builder*, 5 April 1912). This was primarily an exercise in town-planning rather than house-building. Falkner's design incorporated many features to regulate motor vehicles—a bypass, one-way streets, traffic restrictions in the town-centre—which were fifty years before their time. In third place was Patrick Abercrombie who later became Britain's foremost town planner.

In 1913 he submitted, along with 196 other leading architects of the day, a design in the *Country Life* competition for a country house in Sussex. Although he did not win one of the prizes, his design was singled out for favourable comment by Lawrence Weaver, one of the judges.

War memorials were a staple for architects in the period after the First World War. In their obituary *The Builder* noted that Falkner had been placed second in war memorial competitions at Southport and Portsmouth. His sketch of Lutyens' Cenotaph at Whitehall was the frontispiece of the *Architects' Journal* for 13 August 1919. The following month he had an article published in *The Architectural Review* suggesting a design for an RAF memorial on the Embankment in London.

The biggest British architectural project of the inter-war years was the building of a new Indian capital at New Delhi, first announced in 1911 but not completed until 1930. Many architects hoped it would be the subject of a competition but it was captured from the start by HF's old acquaintance Edwin Lutyens, with some input from Herbert Baker (who had done similar work in South Africa) and Reginald Blomfield (Falkner's old mentor, President of RIBA in 1912). The work prompted a flurry of interest among Indian princes for employing English architects to build them new palaces. It may have been in this context that Falkner experimented with oriental designs: his water-colours of 'Designs for an Eastern Potentate' were published in the *Architects' Journal* of 21 October 1925.

In 1927, together with his partner G.M. Aylwin, he was placed third in the Nottingham Market Place Competition, primarily an exercise in site layout rather than building. It would have given him pleasure that *The Builder* of 18 November 1927 gave their designs two full pages rather than the single page devoted to the winner.

In 1931 he took part in the competition for a cathedral at Guildford. Out of 170 architects taking part, his design (see Plate XV) was ranked in the top ten, though not selected for the final five who were awarded £500 to complete more detailed plans. The competition was finally won by a simplified Gothic design in brick by Sir Edward Maufe but not completed until 1966. Falkner was always highly indignant that he had costed his design at £4 million, whereas Maufe had estimated his at £1 million—and it ended up costing over £9 million. It was a similar story to his first disappointment in not winning the design for the council offices in Farnham in 1901. Falkner's design for Guildford looks impressively Gothic but might have been difficult for him to execute. He hung the drawing in his hallway, together with another of his competition entry for the main buildings of Southampton University.

As architectural historian

Falkner was, of course, the foremost authority on the architectural history of Farnham, always ready with an opinion about the origins of any building. Mention has already been made of his historical detective work uncovering earlier versions of Moor Park House outside the town, and of the *Goats Head* and the Bailiffs' Hall at the centre of town. His article on Farnham, published in *The Architectural Review*, September 1916, is a classic of its kind: nine pages of scholarly historical research, leavened with some humour, and illustrated with several of his pencil sketches. *The Architectural Review* commissioned him to write several articles of this sort: on Bath (1910), Lyme Regis (1910), Bradford-on-Avon (1918), and Oxford (1920). These articles focus on the problems of modernising old towns, and encompass the full range of civic building, medieval as well as Georgian, and traffic and town planning.

His special interest was in Georgian buildings, but he was not by nature a joiner and never participated in the Georgian Group which was founded as a result of the destruction of the Adelphi. Although his main interest was in pre-19th-century buildings, he wrote appreciatively of the late Victorian architect Norman Shaw:

'He raised domestic architecture out of the slough of despond in which he found it. He lived through two generations, and having got as far as he could go in one revival, he abandoned it, and for years easily led another. We must not judge him by our contemporaries, but by his own. We profit by his mistakes and by his triumphs, as another generation will profit by ours. But do not let us make the mistake of supposing that we should be where we are if Norman Shaw had not done the spade-work and set his ladders against the walls of the Philistines.'[3]

He was so absorbed by Shaw that in 1915, while serving in the army as a Corporal in Ireland, he sent Reginald Blomfield a package of Shaw drawings: 'I have a number of Norman Shaw original drawings and put them in a box consigned to RIBA for safe-keeping … trusting they will accept them and they may be accessible to students and others.'[4] In 1932 he sent RIBA a further package of plans, drawings and photographs of Shaw's Bank in Farnham, with a covering letter describing the ingenious way in which Shaw had used steel girders ('another new toy of 1868'), fitting them into the oak and brick. He surveyed the bank in detail, noting the complexity of the plan. In 1940, at the advanced age of 85, his mentor Sir Reginald Blomfield published a book on Norman Shaw, which prompted Falkner to contribute a four-page article on the subject in *Country Life* (15 March 1941), under the title 'The Creator of Modern Queen Anne'. The tone was complimentary to both men, and tinged with Falkner's own regret at being party to the demolition of Shaw's Knights Bank in Farnham in 1933 (albeit that he had recorded it in his sketches and managed to save some of the plans).

His architectural reminiscences, from which I have quoted so extensively in Chapter 2, are a classic: historical, perceptive and humorous, never pompous or self-satisfied. This explains their reproduction in those pillars of the architectural press *The Architects' Journal* (1938) and *The Builder* (1944). Over the course of a long career he had had contact with all the main British architectural movements from 1890 to 1960.

Falkner grew up only a few miles away from Lutyens, who had been born at Thursley six years earlier, and had studied Lutyens' first country house at Crooksbury and his first public building, the Liberal Club in Farnham. They were each close friends of Gertrude Jekyll, and wrote about her at length. When Christopher Hussey produced a definitive biography of Lutyens in 1951, Falkner wrote to him:

> 'I have been reading your biography of Lutyens with great interest. Of course, no-one gives a hoot for Lutyens now, thanks to leaders in architectural thought (of which you must count yourself as one).
>
> 'In 1895 Chapman decided to enlarge his house [at Crooksbury, Lutyens' first major house commission, which Falkner had criticised as 'nothing to write home about']. Lutyens produced a building which was a revelation. It had not the least relation to the existing and turned its back on it. It foreshadowed everything that Lutyens was to become. A perfect mastery of materials, a most ingenious plan, a serene front looking out onto the stone paved terrace and garden …'[5]

Today, his views are especially interesting for the light they shed on the connection between the Arts and Crafts movement of 1880-1910 and European Modernism of 1920-1960. In the context of architecture the theorists of both movements could claim common ideological roots going back, in an English context, to Morris and Ruskin—and yet the older movement worshipped the individual craftsman whereas the newer one worshipped the machine. The synthesis between the two was provided by Nikolaus Pevsner's book *Pioneers of the Modern Movement, from William Morris to Walter Gropius* which was written only two years after he had fled from Hitler's Germany to England in 1934. Pevsner passionately believed in Modernism as it had been practised in Germany by the Bauhaus Group, and, scholarly art historian as he was, sought to provide it with a pedigree and connect it with earlier ideas in England.

As a socialist himself, Pevsner could respect the socialist ideals of Morris. He went further, by emphasising what he believed to be the moral superiority of egalitarianism. He shared Morris' belief in the architect as an agent of change; and went beyond it in seeing the architect as a social engineer, and in being prepared to sweep away much of the old (albeit that he was himself the foremost architectural historian of the day) in order to transform society. He also shared Morris' belief in 'truth and honesty' in architecture. This could take several different forms. First, the idea that the outside of a building should 'honestly' reflect its internal layout, which should in turn be dictated by its function rather than any need for symmetry in a facade. Second, the idea of 'truth to materials', a belief that a building should not disguise the materials it was made of—such as pretending that steel beams were wood. Third, an aversion to restoring old buildings with anything less than total historical accuracy.

Another aspect of honesty, espoused more strongly by Pevsner who had grown up with the German concept of the Zeitgeist, was a perceived need for architecture to be 'an honest expression of the spirit of the age'. For Pevsner the 'spirit of the age' incorporated democracy, socialism, a willingness to innovate and a belief in progress. He had little respect for those architects such as Lutyens who were not, in his opinion, 'true' to it. Morris, brought up in the Puritan tradition, thought that simplicity was virtuous, and that elaboration in architecture, as developed since the Renaissance, was bad. The Arts and Crafts movement was against clutter indoors, and in favour of fresh air. All these were moral imperatives for Pevsner and the Modernists. There was thus much common ground between the Arts and Crafts and the Modernists, but it was still difficult to gloss over, in the context of England, their opposing attitudes to history and to the machine. Falkner's voice of common sense was an embarrassment here.

In the first place he adhered to the ideals of Ruskin and of Morris that memory was an important aspect of architecture, not in the sense of evoking classical mythology as had been so prevalent in the 18th century, but in the sense of linking the work of the past with the present and, through new craftsmanship, with the future. For the Arts and Crafts movement history in architecture was an aspect of national identity, to be lovingly preserved where old buildings existed, and carried forward by new buildings when they were created. On the other hand the Modernist architects regarded history as irrelevant, and the past as something to be rejected. Pevsner inveighed against 'historicism', by which he meant an imitation of the past, and in favour of the idea that Modernist architecture should be wholly about the present.

In the second place there was the divergence of view about the machine. Falkner was not by nature anti-machine—he loved cars and planes and motor-cycles—and he could sympathise with the Bauhaus approach which began teaching building with learning how to saw wood and lay bricks. But he had a habit of pointing out that architectural style was largely a matter of ephemeral taste whereas both the Arts and Crafts architects and the Modernists insisted that they were Movements rather than mere Fashions, and represented Progress.

The architectural establishment, which was dominated by Modernism in the period 1925-65, was represented by the Royal Institute of British Architects. Ever since its foundation in the early 19th century distinguished architects had quarrelled with it; indeed it was almost a tradition for architects to rebel against conformity or to squabble among themselves. This applied not only to younger architects but also to older ones, such as Lutyens who resigned in a huff in 1930. Aylwin did Falkner, who had never sat any RIBA examinations, a favour in getting him elected a Fellow in 1928. He was happy to add FRIBA to his notepaper, but in the 1930s he quarrelled increasingly with the membership department, refusing to pay his subscription and ultimately resigning over RIBA's sponsorship of a Bauhaus exhibition.

In a letter to the *Architects' Journal*, 24 January 1935, he explained his views on Beauty in Architecture. He said he could understand the worship of the machine, describing how when he was in the First World War he thought a new propeller very ugly, but after it had performed well in tests he suddenly thought it the most beautiful thing he had ever seen.

> 'So with cars: look at a second hand shop with four or five year old models. What a sight! Can anyone really have admired these clumsy old relics? Yet their owners thought them so lovely … So it is with all machines, and will be with these mechanical contrivances now called "modern architecture". In a few years they will be duds and, worse still, jokes. … Beauty has very little to do with utility, and nothing with economy. If these were the tests, the speculative builders' semi-detached houses would be the high-water mark of taste.
>
> ' …What then is beauty in architecture? In the first place it must have a seemliness in relation to its surroundings … its proportion must be pleasing … Its material must be well-chosen. …It must be permanent, there is no such thing as temporary architecture. … It may have individuality (kept in strict subordination to rule one). … It had better have some considerable adaptability to its purpose [or it will not survive]. It may have ornament. If the designer is a genius it may have functionalism.'

In the *Architects' Journal* of 7 October 1937 he wrote a piece (after a note suggesting it was about time they "hedged on modernism") under the heading 'CHROMIUM TUBING IS AS DEAD AS MUTTON'. Principally a defence of Edwardian architecture, it deals with the tricky question of 'Taste'. Here Falkner's views are very much with William Morris in his praise of individual craftsmanship and against machine-made materials such as chromium tubing. He was sceptical about the 1905 'wave from the Continent, l'Art Nouveau, which swept some of our younger brethren off their feet … and died as quickly as it came, and as the 1930s 'Modernism' will die. … The things which should be preserved are designed by the people who make them; no-one can sit down at a board to design a thing to be made by a machine and achieve beauty ...'

In 1938 he had a public debate in the *Architects' Journal* with Professor C.H. Reilly, Professor of Architecture at Liverpool (whom Falkner described, with tongue in cheek, as 'one of the most respected authorities in the world'). He wrote (28 April issue):

> 'Just over forty years ago I first met C.H. Reilly, as he then was, red-headed, full of energy and ideas. It was at Walter Crane's house, and after dinner we were going on to the Academy 'soiree'; after which I lost the last train and walked some twenty miles home. I was invited because I was a joint pupil with Lionel Crane with Mr (now Sir) Reginald Blomfield. ... I may then have been a spectator at the inception of a movement which has led, for better or worse, to considerable developments, some of which are not completely understood by commentators of the present day.'

He went on to describe the pioneers of the Arts and Crafts movement (as quoted in Chapter 1 of this book) and to remark that architectural criticism was practically unknown at that time:

> 'Whether the lack of architectural criticism was the cause or not who shall say, but the stuff these 'eminent' gentlemen turned out was truly awful ...The mistake architectural critics of today make is in supposing that nobody knew it; everyone did; even the subjects themselves, but they were the heads of flourishing 'businesses' not to be lightly thrown away.'

He described the schism in the RIBA between those who favoured exams and those who did not, and the tendency of the architectural schools, the Architectural Association (Liverpool among them), to

> 'mob-psychology, to be easily swept away by fleeting fashion. ... All the revivals were failing or had failed'—and the Arts and Crafts movement did not take their place because of 'its antagonism to commercial ideas. When it pleased Herr Hitler to export non-Aryan architects the movement was received back into Britain with open arms, but by a strange irony of circumstance (the post-war economy) the principal material in Germany had been concrete. With this most uninspiring substance and steel (which in Britain was unnaturally cheap) and glass, and chromium plate, and dyed aluminium all 'bright and attractive' allied to the new sanitarian craze for 'light and yet more light', Functionalism and Modernism caught on.
>   ' ... Here was heaven-sent emancipation: "Away with the orders, the styles, architectural history, the dusty museums, let every boy or girl design from his own inner consciousness or temperamental inclination". ... It may be encouraging to the young to tell them that what their predecessors have done for the past fifty years is tripe and copyism, but is it wise to let it spread to the man-in-the-street?'

The Professor replied (*Architects' Journal*, 23 June 1938):

I still think it was necessary in 1904 to clear up the mess of Falkner's Arts and Crafts friends … by a clean mature classic. We learnt refinement by doing so. A sound knowledge of classical architecture for the modern designer is essential. The general and thorough use of steel is the main reason for our changed way of thinking. May you live long enough, dear Falkner, to design big jobs with lots of steel and to show in them that you, too, have made an honest man of yourself.

Falkner wrote in the same issue:

'The Arts and Crafts movement of 1890-1914 was not my property. I was but a humble member of the junior branch. Morris was the founder, the permeating spirit and sustainer, and the classicists were only allowed in on sufferance, and provided they swallowed large doses of craftsmanship at frequent intervals.

'I agree with the Professor, it is very difficult to see how the student is to be trained to produce this "best modern work". I go further, I cannot tell when he (or she) has been so trained. Anyone can do it.

' … The Professor is not fair to my colleagues: we do not "copy". Because I use bricks and tiles and sash windows (when my clients can afford them) it doesn't say I copy. I grew up in a town where every house (above £50 rateable) has sash windows with bars. The conditions under which my clients live are as nearly as possible identical with those of the original inhabitants of the houses. Why should I use anything else?

' … The Professor has been out of touch with the practical side of building: two or three "consultation" jobs make very little difference. … He tells us that two of the authors of the most "advanced" buildings are enthusiastic admirers of the old Georgian; I am not surprised. It must make a nice change after looking at their own work.'

For many years Falkner corresponded with Nikolaus Pevsner. In a final letter (quoted by Pevsner in his obituary) Falkner wrote:

'We approach the business [of architecture] from extreme opposites, and consequently don't come to the same conclusion. We do agree however on one point: that English architecture at certain periods led the world, that the First World War nearly killed it, that the Second War completed the job, and that the influx of continental influences and the schools disturbed the corpse but did not raise it.

'You and your fellow journalists are delighted to get away from something which takes a lot of understanding and even experience … in the hope of finding something new. For thirty years you have been looking and have found nothing.'

CHAPTER NINE

Epilogue

Falkner in Old Age

Falkner had never been conventional, and towards the end of his life he became increasingly shabby and eccentric. He played to this image, but remained energetic and never became senile. Anecdotes abound about him as a sort of tramp with a succession of battered felt hats, bought second-hand or bought new and with the rim cut off. He was never without his hat. When he left it in Bristol it was sent on to him; when his car caught fire he used it to extinguish the flames—and the soot remained: the *Farnham Herald* suggested he should buy a new one at a jumble sale where hats were priced at a penny each. In wearing a hat at all he was, of course, a throwback to a previous generation, but in being careless about his appearance he was more in tune with modern architectural students.

55 'Mr Harold Falkner considering the problem of a NEW HAT', sketch by Sir John Verney.

His bad leg became worse, making it difficult to climb stairs or drive his car. A defect in one eye led to his carrying a white stick: he would tap his way along the pavement like a blind man, then get into his car and drive off at speed. He was often seen waving his white stick out of the car window telling people to get out of his way as he could not stop—which was probably true. At one stage he could only get out of his bath by filling it to the brim and then floating out, flooding his house in the process. Increasingly he looked unwashed, even when visiting friends' houses. He said he had his car sprayed a mottled grey so that it would not show the dirt. He probably enjoyed, as old men often do, being considered an eccentric, 'a character'. But the anecdotes, like any caricature, miss out on his essential humanity, his kindness, his enterprise, and the fact that even in old age his mind remained sharp.

In his house in West Street, formerly meticulously maintained by a housekeeper,[1] he lived a disorganised life. He never drew the curtains at night, which meant that passers-by could see in and notice the chaos inside. A chess board was always set up in the living room: he had several regular opponents in the town—the teenage son of a local solicitor, the artist Tom Luzny who was also one of his tenants, and the Superintendent of the Farnham police. The kitchen was covered with remains of his breakfast, lunch and tea. There were piles of old issues of *Country Life*, and his belongings were in a permanent muddle. He ceased to use the upstairs rooms: Nigel Temple recalls going into one where there was a corona of woodworm dust around each piece of Chippendale furniture.

Amid all this he continued to write to the press, both local and national. The press continued to publish him, although, as Aylwin remarked, he had the distinction of being a person whose typing was almost illegible: a typical opening was 'My Dear Hock?£#'.

For long car trips he relied on lifts from friends. Young solicitor's clerk Owen Crundwell drove with him on expeditions to find the architectural salvage which he used for re-cycling. A favourite destination was Crowther's of Syon Lodge; notable items could always be found there, but Falkner also enjoyed finding derelict salvage himself. Nigel Temple, who had just published one book on Farnham's buildings (*Farnham Inheritance*, 1956) and was working on his next (*Farnham Buildings and People*, 1963) took him to visit the great country houses of the surrounding area, such as Uppark, Mottisfont, Petworth, Avington Park and The Vyne. A particular favourite was Marsh Court, built by Lutyens 1901-04 with a garden by Gertrude Jekyll; the combination naturally appealed to Falkner, and visits were facilitated by the fact that the wife of the principal of the school there was the daughter of an old Farnham friend.

Nigel Temple also introduced him to the benefits of projected 35mm colour slides for architectural study. Falkner retained his capacious knowledge of architecture, and enjoyed debating aspects of architectural history. He often argued with the guide who was showing them around a building. At Uppark she suggested that Georgian windows had small glazing panes because it was not possible at the time to make large sheets of glass—to which Falkner expostulated: 'What about those large mirrors?' He claimed that the angles of white glazing bars in windows were designed (together with the angle of the shutters) to reflect light into a room.

Every week he walked down West Street to attend the nearby Castle Theatre.

> He had a great love of the theatre and most Saturday nights at 8 o'clock would find him at the tiny Theatre in Castle Street. Owing to his game leg he would not arrive until the last minute, and often, just as I had shut the door and drawn the door curtains, he would come stumping across the foyer, thrust me his ticket and descend the three steps to the front row where he always had a seat. Once there, he would rest his leg on the low stage and often proceed to eat his supper out of a newspaper. One evening he cut bread and cheese with a knife with a bell on it, to the discomfiture of the players and the amusement of the audience. Going home one night he was given a half-crown by a well-meaning passer-by, which much upset the old gentleman![2]

Such actions and stories amused the ordinary people of Farnham, albeit that they were slightly in awe of him. To a young person like Brian Haworth, whom he employed as a sixteen-year old to copy drawings, he was kind and avuncular. The old man left him alone, apart from his pleasant full-time housekeeper, in the big front room at 24 West Street to make full-size drawings of joinery and brickwork. When Haworth was subsequently apprenticed to G.M. Aylwin he often ran across him in the cafe opposite 24 West Street, and Falkner was affable enough.

He was less popular with the professional people of the town. In his case the usual 'maturing' process was reversed. In his youth he had been broadly conventional in his views, swimming along with the Arts and Crafts movement and despising high Victorianism, and deferential to those in authority even where he saw their faults—a contrast to 20th-century architectural students who usually pride themselves on being iconoclastic and *avant-garde*. It was in his later years that he became an *enfant terrible*, delighting in upsetting establishment figures.

After the death of Borelli in 1950 his lack of tact and persuasive skills became more apparent. He could be rude, intemperate, and unreasonable. He quarrelled with business contacts, lawyers and planners, local government officials, and anyone in a position of authority. The Town Council became exasperated with him. James Hockey, Principal of the Art School, described him as a 'dangerous man' to Alan Windsor who discovered how awkward Falkner could be when he became his tenant; nevertheless both men had great respect for his artistic talent and helped rescue his drawings which had been thrown away after his death.

Like many men in their eighties, Falkner outlived his local contemporaries. He had been greatly saddened by the death of Borelli, and of his last loyal worker, Alfred Hack, who fell to his death from one of his buildings in Dippenhall. Of his employees the only survivor was A.J. Lehman, who had done clerical work for him for forty years.

His domestic chores were looked after by Alfred Hack's daughter. She did his shopping, prepared his lunch, and struggled to keep order in the house, at least in the downstairs rooms—'the upper floors were too full of junk to do much about'. When she was ill, her daughter came to help: she has fond memories of 'a lovely

56 Harold Falkner at eighty-seven.

old man, kind and knowledgeable, who was so upset when mother had to go into hospital'. In his will Falkner left her Yew Tree Cottage in Old Church Lane, owned by him but for long the Hack family home.

After his death, Sir John Verney, a fellow resident of Farnham who knew him well, wrote a novel, *Fine Day for a Picnic*, about an eccentric 86-year-old architect who devoted his life to preserving the 'essential character' of an old town; 'while he was developing a nice line in country houses round the perimeter, he had fought to keep the centre largely unaltered—except of course by himself.' The book is dedicated to Harold Falkner and is an affectionate portrait of him as raconteur, chess enthusiast, a kindly eccentric, and a determined conservationist of both trees and old buildings who describes modern architecture as engineering rather than architecture, 'match boxes stuck together, skeletons rather than the sinews and flesh which make architecture interesting'. The signs on the wall of the Council Offices Planning Committee advise that in this town, 'Three storeys are the maximum' and 'Pitched roofs are right'. The book makes the point that while his efforts to preserve the heart of the old town had been successful, there had developed a balloon of suburban building to the south and west where planning restrictions discouraged shops—and in the long run, long after his death, the old architect's land is used to build a new University.

Since John Verney's book was written, the Surrey Institute of Art and Design has been founded in Farnham, developing out of the original Farnham School of Art where Falkner studied a century earlier. It now has several thousand students and university status. The road which leads to it is called Falkner Road.

His contemporary and obituarist A.J. Stevens put his eccentricities into perspective:[3]

> His clothes matched his hat, and to see him with great agility extricate himself from his old ark and start to hobble along determinedly with an elbow-crutch and stick, you would think 'Well, of all the disreputable old tramps that have ever been, this is the archetype'—and how completely wrong you would be.
>
> Removal of his scarecrow hat would set free a flowing mass of white hair over a high forehead and what had been as handsome a face as has been my lot to meet. The shape of his one-time perfect aquiline nose was somewhat marred when he drove into the end of some scaffold poles carried by the vehicle in

front of him, so foreshortened he was unaware of it. In earlier years his eyes were very striking and bright and unerringly observant, and the natural dignity of the whole man was such that it would not have mattered if he wore twenty scarecrow hats; he was always entirely himself in any place and in any company. All this had no suggestion of showmanship, but was merely a natural expression of his sense of values.

He was endowed with exceptional brains—brilliant and remarkably quick— one result of which was that he anticipated what anyone addressing him meant to convey long before the sentence was finished, showing this by saying 'Yes, yes, yes' very quickly in his characteristic manner. ... He certainly would not suffer fools gladly, nor had he any hesitation in calling a spade a spade.

He was abstemious, without being an actual teetotaller, with regard to both alcohol and tobacco ... What he said was well worth listening to in almost any connection: for his memory was amazing considering the ground he covered in his reading, which was wide and must have been consistently and quietly continued throughout his life. ... He built up a picture of how and why things were done more vividly than I have ever read of them. He had strong and well-founded views on painting, literature, sociology and gardening. ... Indeed, a man of very memorable parts. ... With [all] that he had a deep-seated generosity ... He was, if in general remote, a most kindly and loveable man.

Harold Falkner died on 30 November 1963, two days after his 88th birthday.

His bequests

Despite his image as a tramp, Falkner died a rich man owning land and property in Farnham, Frensham and Dippenhall. His antique furniture and oil paintings were valuable—one picture sold for £4,200—and his total estate was assessed for Death Duties at £114,000.

A major beneficiary under his will was the Farnham Society, to which he left his house and furniture at 24 West Street and his half share of Wickham House in West Street (the other half being owned by the executors of C.E. Borelli).

His wish was that the Society, which he had helped to found in 1911, would open a museum for Georgian and earlier objects in one of these two houses. Due to lack of financial resources the Society was unable to do this. Two years after his death 24 West Street was sold to Surrey County Council for £9,000, and used for many years as additional accommodation for the Art School next door. Subsequently it was used as hostel accommodation for students at the Surrey Institute of Art and Design. In 2001 it was restored and refurbished by a private company and became the office of WhiteOaks Consultancy, a public relations firm, and Arcadia, a property development firm.

Advice on the refurbishment was given by the Museum of Farnham and The Farnham Society. In 1968 members of the Society founded the Farnham (Building Preservation) Trust to take up Falkner's concern for preserving the older buildings of Farnham. Since then they have rescued many old buildings in the town and restored them for modern use.

Other beneficiaries under his will were the descendants of his brother Charles. Male descendants were to receive more than the girls, and it was a condition that if his great-niece became the sole heir and married, then her husband should take the name of Falkner.

Falkner's architectural legacy

Nikolaus Pevsner wrote his obituary in *The Architectural Review*, beginning: 'The room at the back of a house in the main street of Farnham in which we had tea with Harold Falkner in 1960 was nauseatingly slummy. His hands were so dirty that they made us shudder. But it was his house and—cursing away at mid-twentieth century life and modern architecture—he was probably happy.' For an obituary, where the custom is to say nothing but good, this was hardly complimentary, but the fact that the obituary was written by Pevsner, doyen of architectural historians and the Modern Movement of which Falkner was the enemy, is itself significant.

There has never been any doubt that the people of Farnham are grateful to him for the appearance of the town today. As A.J. Stevens pointed out, they owe him more than the other two Farnham worthies who became nationally famous, William Cobbett and George Sturt. Now the shadow of Modernism has shifted, he can be seen on the national stage as an original and inventive architect who was also a real craftsman in the medieval and Arts and Crafts traditions. He has a simple grave in the West Street cemetery, but a Farnham citizen might quote Wren's epitaph in the crypt of St Paul's cathedral: 'If you require to see his monument, look around you'.

Many of Falkner's buildings, particularly the neo-Georgian, are often dismissed as mere pastiche. This is unfair. He did not build sham buildings, he re-created them. Either by stripping them back to something approaching their original design, or by applying old design principles to new buildings, or by imaginative use of old materials. He was an early re-cycler of architectural salvage, which is today such big business. Many times he would strip a building back to its origins, and then re-create it sympathetically.

Falkner himself robustly disagreed with the suggestion that his buildings were pastiche. He was convinced that old styles were the best, expostulating that he did not build 'mock-Georgian' any more than he baked a 'mock' apple pie when he used a tried and tested recipe. It is a tribute to his skill that so often his buildings have confounded experts on old buildings: his carving is so realistically antique, his materials are often so genuinely old, and the way he puts them together so difficult to distinguish from the real thing, that many experts on old buildings have been 'fooled by Falkner'. Even his ideological opponents among contemporary architectural critics, such as Nikolaus Pevsner and Ian Nairn, acknowledged his skill. In his obituary, Pevsner noted that 'Nairn, whom no-one can accuse of believing in shams, went out of his way to praise Falkner's imitations.'

While he was still in his 20s his designs were often chosen for exhibition at the Royal Academy, starting with his *Designs for Urban District Council Offices in a*

Small Country Town (1900). Up to the First World War, his ideas and designs were broadly in tune with his contemporaries, but he never came to terms with the Modern Movement which came to dominate architectural thought after 1920. He clung defiantly to the old idea that architecture was more an art than engineering and should take account of tradition and decoration; he detested flat roofs and modern materials and stark simplicity. As a result his appearances ceased in *The Architectural Review*, standard bearer for the Modern Movement, though the other architectural journals still gave him space as a link to the past.

It was his misfortune that although his early work was broadly in line with architectural thought of the time, much of his working life was spent under the shadow of the Modern Movement, and yet only a few years after his death Robert Venturi in America and Aldo Rossi in Italy were suggesting that there might, after all, be merit in architecture having a consciousness of the past. In 1968 an article in *The Architectural Review*, which had ostracised him for the past 45 years, described his Dippenhall buildings as works of a genius. The pendulum had swung and much of what Falkner did and said is now, 40 years after his death, more admired than it was during his lifetime.

He began his career as an Arts and Crafts man, as one might expect from someone who had studied under the influence of Morris. He later developed, particularly for the exteriors, a preference for Queen Anne and Georgian styles, though he never abandoned the Arts and Crafts principles with which he had trained. As he grew older he became increasingly interested in older buildings, culminating in his eccentric barn reconstructions at Dippenhall. In this sense his development was the reverse of Lutyens, who began with the traditional architecture of rural Surrey, designing country houses with an Arts and Crafts flavour, and ended his career with neo-classical buildings of regular symmetry, normally in the centre of cities.

Throughout his life, and especially in his later years, he was fiercely independent and scathing about fashionable trends. This was partly a reflection of his own character, but also made easier by the fact that his personal finances (and perhaps also his lack of a wife) enabled him to be so. Unlike most architects, he did not, at least in his later work, have to depend on meeting the wishes of his clients, and he had no respect for any architectural critics who were not also 'hands-on' builders.

He may have seemed a reactionary, but in fact he had a modern sympathy for scale and grouping and the urban environment. The appearance of Farnham town centre today is an important part of his architectural legacy, both the buildings in which he was involved and the ones which he and Borelli saved from destruction. Their concern for local architectural heritage was fifty years before its time, although, spurred by organisations such as SAVE Britain's Heritage (founded 1975), it is now considered normal.

Location of Falkner Buildings in Farnham

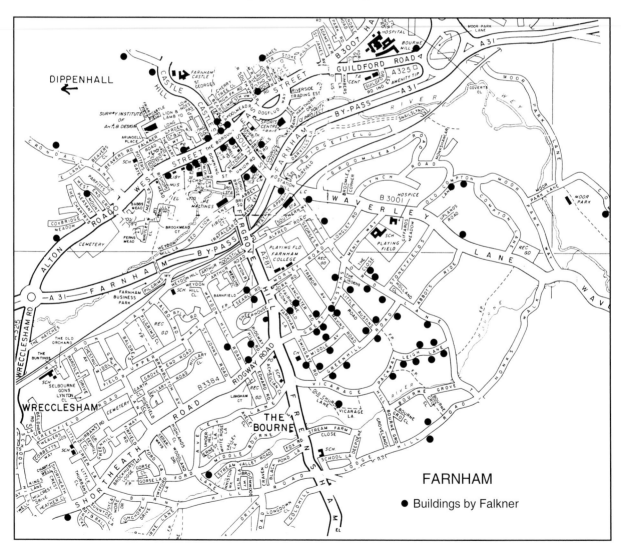

Buildings by Harold Falkner

(About 30 commercial buildings and about 85 houses)
This is a list of buildings with which Harold Falkner was involved, either as main architect or as a contributor (e.g. in his partnerships with Niven and Wigglesworth, and later with Aylwin). As he left few records a definitive attribution is often problematic. The following abbreviations have been used:

FM   Included in a list of Falkner buildings, compiled c.1970, held in Farnham Museum.

WHB   Included in List of Buildings of Local Architectural or Historic Interest in Farnham Area, compiled by the Historic Buildings Section of Waverley Borough Council, 1995.

BF   Attributed to Falkner by his niece Beryl Falkner.

??   Falkner attribution or involvement is possible but unsubstantiated.

*   Reconstruction/additions by HF to an older building.

Central Farnham

* 1 West Street [corner with Downing Street]. Alliance pub rebuilt by HF and Aylwin 1929 for Courage Ltd. FM
* 6 and 6A West Street. FM. Listed Gr II.
* 20A West Street — new shopfront by HF (and 17th-century ceiling uncovered) Listed Gr II.
* 24 West Street. The Falkner family home: bathroom added in 1897 by HF.
* 40 West Street (Wickham House). 18th-century house remodelled by HF and Aylwin. Listed Gr II.
* 104A West Street. Late Georgian shopfront (or 19th-century copy) brought by HF from London, and set behind 'giraffe arches'. FM. Listed Gr II.
* 114 and 115 West Street [Farnham Herald office]. HF shopfront 1952. FM. Listed Gr II.
17 West End Grove. *Architectural Review* May 1906 [shown at Royal Academy]. Since enlarged. FM.
'Cottage for Mr F. Sturt' *Architectural Review* May 1901, *Builders' Journal* 9/10/1901. Not built?
Sampson's Almshouses, West Street (opposite west gate of cemetery). 1933-34. FM.

* *Bush Hotel*, The Borough. Old coaching inn extended by HF and Aylwin. HF installed chimney from Knights Bank 1934. Listed Gr II.
??* 5-7 The Borough. Georgian buildings reconstructed in 1915 by Horace Field (possibly prompted by Borelli/Falkner).
* 10 The Borough [corner with Castle St, now a travel agent]. FM. Listed Gr II*.

* 40 The Borough [Spinning Wheel, formerly Goat's Head Inn, late 16th-century]. FM. Listed Gr II.

??* 41/42 The Borough. Tudor facade *c.*1920, not removed when Boots moved there *c.*1930.

Town Hall buildings. 1930-34 by HF and Aylwin. Listed Gr II.

* Bailiffs Hall, next to Town Hall in The Borough. Fine 17th-century brickwork by HF. FM. Listed Gr II.

Lloyds Bank, Castle Street. Not designed by HF, but he was instrumental in this 1931 replacement of Norman Shaw's Knights Bank building.

* 94 and 95 East Street. Shopfront inserted by HF. Whole building now demolished. FM.

Seven Stars, East Street. Pub rebuilt 1929 by HF and Aylwin in Tudor style. FM. *Farnham Herald* 28 Dec. 1990.

Electric Theatre [later County Cinema], 8 East St. 1913. Demolished 1956. FM.

17 South Street [corner with Victoria Road]. 1915, for Farnham Art School (now a solicitor's office). FM.

Old Swimming Bath entrance, Brightwells Road. 1897 (Queen's Diamond Jubilee). WHB p.16.

Gostrey Meadow. 1910 overall layout as a public park by HF, who also designed the drinking fountain and the shelter with a column by the playground.

* *Blue Boy* [previously *Railway Hotel*, now *The Exchange*] additions by HF and Aylwin 1929. Listed Gr II.

* *Waverley Arms*, Waverley Lane. Pub remodelled by HF and Aylwin 1931.

St Joan of Arc church, Tilford Road. 1929-34 by Nicholas and Dixon-Spain. WHB p.70. Some HF/GMA input via Borelli. *Architectural Design and Construction* Feb. 1937.

Pilgrims' Way Motorworks [later the Plasmec factory], Weydon Lane, 1905. *Farnham Herald*, 13 March 1987. Demolished 1990.

* Bourne Mill 17th-18th-century. Bought by HF, refurbished and split into flats 1958 [ref. M.H. Garrood, *Farnham Herald*, 21 Nov. 1997]. Now an antique shop.

Houses in North Farnham
Falcon [originally Knole] House, Old Park Lane. HF and Aylwin 1929. FM.

Bishops Square, Castle Hill (adjoining Old Park Lane). Neo-Georgian by HF and Aylwin 1928. [previously Park Lane House, originally 'Hill House for Major-General Sir Edward Perceval'].

* Pilgrim's Way, Crondall Lane. Old farmhouse with wing and staircase added by HF *c.*1929.

?? Deer Leap, 1 St James Terrace.

?? Semi-detached houses in Osborne Road (similar to the HF cottages on The Ridgway): numbers 1 and 3, 5 and 7, 9 and 11, 2 and 4, 6 and 8.

Houses in South Farnham — Great Austins area
Blue Cedars, opposite 86 Tilford Road. FM.

Strangers Corner, 88 Tilford Road. 1897/1902. FM. WHB p.70. Built for HF's art master.

Great Austins House, 90 Tilford Road. Converted *c.*1970 with many flats and houses behind. *Builders' Journal* 27/6/1906. FM. Outbuilding WHB p.71.

Fairywood [originally Margreig], Tilford Road. 1911. Split into two [Buckland House and Robin Hey]. *Country Life* (supplement) 4/1/1913. FM. WHB p.71.

Headon Cottage, The Close off Tilford Road. Site redeveloped 1996 but original cottage retained. FM.

Mavins End, 2 Greenhill Road [split with Mavins House]. 1927. Garden 1925 by Gertrude Jekyll. Listed Gr II. FM.
Mavins Court, 4 Greenhill Road. 1906. *Builders' Journal* 24/4/1907.
?? Garden cottage (now 17 Vicarage Hill) to Mavins Court. Built 1920s, extended 1960s.
Montclare House [originally Ilona], 10 Greenhill Road. 1908. *Country Life* 3/9/1910. Listed Gr II. FM.
Tilford Way, 11 Greenhill Road. Split into two (Little Austins end called Beeches). FM.
Delvern [originally Gaywood] House, 13 Greenhill Road (corner with Little Austins). 1905. FM.
* Greenhill Farm and adjoining houses nos 20 and 18, Greenhill Road. *c.*1907 HF conversion by adding an old barn and cottage. Later worked on by others. FM.

Elm Tree Cottage, 10 Great Austins. 1909 for Leo Borelli (brother of Charles). *Country Life* 28 May 1910 (Supplement). FM. WHB p.40.
Lancaster House, 11 Great Austins. Extended in 1980s by former HF pupil Brian Haworth.
Furzedown, 17 Great Austins. *Builders' Journal* 22/2/1911. FM.
The Mount, 19 Great Austins. FM.
Farlands Croft, 20 Great Austins. 1922. Since extended. FM.
The Beeches, 1 Little Austins. 1903. FM.
Orchard House, 7 Little Austins. *Builders' Journal* 21/9/1904. FM. WHB p.47.
10 Little Austins. FM.

Roffey, 2 Middle Avenue. FM. Demolished *c.*1970 and rebuilt as St Thomas' Vicarage.
6 Middle Avenue. 1907? FM.
9 Middle Avenue. 1923? FM.
?? Sherwood, 14 Middle Avenue.
Cobbetts, 1 Mavins Road. 1913. *Country Life* 16 Aug. 1919. FM. WHB p.51.

Shottisham Lodge [formerly Bourne Corner], 7 Swingate Road. 1909. *Architectural Review*, December 1909. FM. WHB p.69.
The Priory, 6 Swingate Road. 1932. Sympathetically extended in 1990s.
Crohamhurst, 16 Lancaster Avenue. FM. Much altered.
Squirrels, 5 Old Farnham Lane. FM. *Builders' Journal* 22/3/1911.

Leigh House, 1 Leigh Lane (corner with Tilford Road). 1908. WHB p.46. *Country Life* (supplement) 4/1/1913.
Leigh House Cottage, 3 Leigh Lane. 1908 (garage/chauffeur for Leigh House), later extended.
Sands Lodge, 2 Leigh Lane (opposite Leigh House).
Sands Cottage, 4 Leigh Lane (garage and chauffeur's cottage for Sands Lodge). Enlarged in 1990s.
Greenhill Brow [originally Costleys], 11 Leigh Lane. 1911. *Country Life* 4/1/1913. *Farnham Herald* 6/9/91. FM. Divided into two (lesser part, with gazebo, called Maple House).
Field Cottage, 7 Leigh Lane (garage and chauffeur's cottage for Costleys).

Green Tubs, The Packway. 1908, sympathetically extended in 1980s. Resembles 'A cottage in Farnham' illustrated in *Builders' Journal* 17/7/1907.

Houses in South Farnham (outside Great Austins area)
Khyber Cottage, 2 Searle Road, off Firgrove Hill. FM.
Cranford, 3 Searle Road, off Firgrove Hill. FM.
Searle House, Firgrove Hill. Rebuilt after war damage.
Cosmar, 70 Firgrove Hill. FM. *Builders' Journal* 22/2/1911.

40/42 and 44/46 Ridgway Road. [two pairs of semi-detached cottages]. FM. WHB p.63.
64 Ridgway Road. 1906. FM.
Rowan Tree Cottage, 1 Ridgeway Hill Road. FM. Later much enlarged.
3 and 5 Ridgway Hill Road. [semi-detached]. *Builders' Journal* 15/3/1905. FM.
90/92 Weydon Hill Road [semi-detached]. FM.
Shortheath Beacon, 95 Shortheath Road. 1903 for HF's sister Mrs Mason. *Academy Architecture*, 1903 p.108.

Lodge Hill House, Lodge Hill Road. 1903. FM. WHB p.48. Long drive. Now divided into three (Bourne House/Huxley House/The Stables).
Merlewood, Lodge Hill Road. 1903. 'House, Lodge Hill, Farnham' in *Academy Architecture*, 1903, pp.37 and 43; and *The Studio* Vol. 36, p.238.

* Stream Cottage, 41 Ford Lane (also has old outbuilding and ironstone wall). Extension by HF (who owned it 1903-39 and occasionally lived there). FM. WHB pp.36/37.
* 5 Old Church Lane. Residence of George Sturt 1891-1927 (plaque). Porch by HF?
Yew Tree Cottage, Old Church Lane. Owned by HF and bequeathed to family of Alfred Hack.

?? Goldhill Place, Goldhill Road. Built *c.*1906 in Arts and Crafts style but no HF provenance.

Houses in East Farnham
The Vyne [originally Gwanda], 12 Old Compton Lane. 1924 for Major H.C. Patrick, funerary stonemason. FM. Site redeveloped 2001, but house (with stone and timber frontage) left intact.
Compton Hill House, 14 Old Compton Lane. 4-acre garden. *Country Life*, 30 Aug. 1919. FM.
Over Compton, 55 Waverley Lane (opposite Abbot's Ride). FM.
Delarden, Moor Park. Large, neo-Georgian. 1938 for local solicitor W.H. Hadfield. FM.
Moor Park House. No HF involvement in the building, but his research highlighted its 17th-century origins. *Country Life*, 25/11/49.

Pictured in national press but not identified:
'Cottage at Farnham' pp.70,71,74 of *Country Cottages* by J. H. Elder-Duncan, 1906.

Houses at Dippenhall:
[ref. *Architectural Review*, Nicholas Taylor, 1968, pp.158-160. *Country Life* 5/1/89 & 6/1/94].
* Dippenhall Grange [formerly Deans farmhouse], remodelled by HF 1920. Gr II Listed.

* Deans Knowe [formerly Deans], Dippenhall Road. 1921 A remodelled cottage. Gr II Listed. FM.

The Barn, Dippenhall Road. 1921. Entrance arch knocked through Barn Cottage. Gr II Listed. FM.

Overdeans Court, Dippenhall Road. 1925. Two barns and stables from Runwick House. Gr II Listed. FM.

Meads, Dora's Green Lane. Two barn frames. 1930-35. Gr II Listed. FM.

Halfway House, Dora's Green Lane. 1934 (split with Old Timbers). FM. WHB p.24.

Burles, off Crondall Lane. Two large barns from Gloucestershire. 1937. Gr II Listed. FM.

Burles Lodge, off Crondall Lane. Georgian style, with folly in the garden. Unfinished at his death. FM

* Grovers Farm, Runwick Lane. HF added neo-Georgian front onto old farmhouse and granary 1960. FM. WHB p.25.

The Old Barn, Runwick Lane [originally Black Barn]. 1960-63, later largely rebuilt. FM. WHB p.25.

Houses outside Farnham (see map overleaf)

* Ripsley House, Liphook. 19th-century house with some HF remodelling. *Builders' Journal* 18 November 1914.

The Chase, Frensham Road (A287), Churt. Long drive, elaborate porch with pilasters. *Builders' Journal*, 19 August 1914. FM. Now divided into three.

?? Hatch Hill House, Churt Road, Hindhead. Neo-Georgian with elaborate porch and cornice. Early 20th-century. Attributed by BF, but owner doubts if HF was the architect.

Sentry Hill, Frensham Green (A287 junction). Since enlarged and modernised, with cottage. FM.

* Hall's Place [previously Hall's Cottage], Woodhill Lane, Frensham. Old cottages converted into house by HF 1923. Jekyll garden. Jacobean gateway.

* The Dial House, Shortfield Common, Millbridge. Old cottage remodelled and enlarged by HF 1904. *Builders' Journal* 17/8/1904. FM.

Crosslanes, Hamlash Lane, Millbridge. Panelling sketched by HF in *Builders' Journal*, 29 August 1906.

The Croft, Hillside Road, Millbridge. 1904. Divided (other part called Moon Cottage). FM.

?? Croft Cottage, 21 Gong Hill Drive, said to have been built by HF c.1908, later divided into four.

Milhanger, Portsmouth Road, Thursley. 1907. Much extended in 1980s. *Builders' Journal*, 15/5/1907; *Academy Architecture*, 1907 p.44. FM

* North Munstead, North Munstead Lane. Conversion of 16th-century cottages into large house for Captain Sampson. *Architects' Journal* 25/3/1925; *Country Life* 6/12/1924. Jekyll garden. FM. Grade II Listed.

Tancreds Ford, The Street (B3001), Tilford. 1913, for Dr Charles Tanner of Farnham. Large. Remodelled 1983 by R. Gradidge and M. Blower. *Country Life* 17 and 24 November 1983.

??* Binton Barn, Botany Hill, The Sands. Now divided into two. Date on the house is
    1892, but BF implied a later alteration by HF.
Greenlees, Furze Road, The Sands. ['House overlooking Farnham Golf Course']. Design
    suggested by HF to Edward Banks. *Architects Journal* 19 Jan. 1939 pp.105-6.
Vere House [originally David's Vere], Binton Lane, The Sands. 1908, much altered c.1979.
    BF. *Builders' Journal* 29 Dec. 1909, p.503; *Architects' Journal* 29 Jun. 1910 pp.666,
    670-3.
The Coach House for Vere House.

Commercial Buildings outside Farnham
Deepcut Dairy Co, Farnborough. *Architectural Review* 1905, pp.176, 177, 180.
    Demolished?
Jolly Farmer, Guildford Road, Runfold. Pub by HF and Aylwin 1932.
Princess Royal, Guildford Road, Runfold. Pub by HF and Aylwin 1931. *Architectural
    Design and Construction*, June 1934.

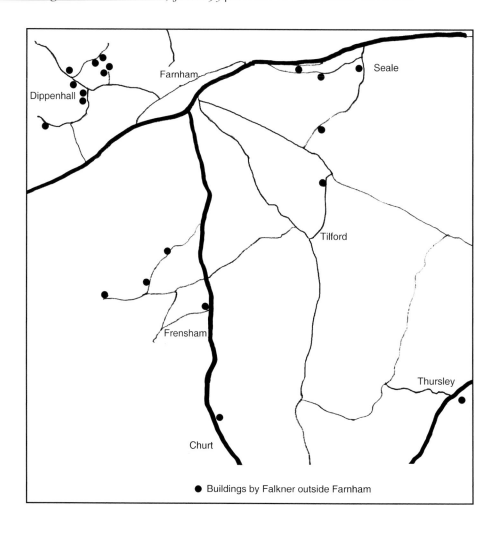

● Buildings by Falkner outside Farnham

Notes

1: British Architecture in 1900
For a fuller summary of the architectural scene in 1900 see pages 3-46 of *Dream Houses* by Roderick Gradidge.
   1. Mark Girouard, *Sweetness and Light: the Queen Anne Movement 1870-1900*, Country Life 1977, p.1.
   2. Which prompted the publication of *The English House 1860-1914* by Gavin Stamp and A.Goulancourt.
   3. 40 years later it was repaired by Bishop Fox (the blind bishop who did so much building at the castle) and is thus also known as Fox's tower.

2: Harold Falkner—The Early Years
   1. Commemorated by a grey and white marble plaque in the south transept of St. Andrew's, Farnham.
   2. Filed with the Ewbank Smith papers in the Museum of Farnham.
   3. The German street bands, and their association with rain, are also described by George Sturt in his book, *A Small Boy in the* [Eighteen] *Sixties*, published in 1927. Sturt was twelve years older than Falkner, but his childhood in Farnham followed a similar pattern—dame school, Grammar School, and Art School.
   4. Leaflet on W.H. Allen by Alice Munro-Faure, 1992, Museum of Farnham.
   5. Quoted in article on Farnham in *Country Life*, 24 July 1942.
   6. Architectural Reminiscences by HF in *The Builder*, 10 November 1944.
   7. Nigel Temple, *Farnham Buildings and People*, p.119.
   8. See 6 above.
   9. *The Architectural Review*, 1964, p.240.
   10. HF Reminiscences in *The Architects' Journal*, 23 June 1938, and *The Builder*, 10 November 1944.
   11. Article by HF in *Bumbledon*, Autumn 1962 (copy in Museum of Farnham).
   12. Article by Christopher Hussey in *Country Life*, 17 July 1942.
   13. *Farnham Herald*, 29 August 1980, p.13.

3: Farnham—The Garden Suburb
   1. *A Short History of The Bourne* by Henry Sidebotham (son of the first Vicar) 1950.
   2. *Edwardian Farnham* by W. Ewbank Smith, p.89.
   3. William Cobbett, *Rural Rides 1826* (Penguin Classics, 1989, p.41).
   4. George Bourne [Sturt], *Change in the Village*, 1985 Edn., pp.58, 110, 160.
   5. Ibid, pp.120-127.
   6. George Sturt *Journals*, for the month of June 1908.
   7. Arthur Mee, *Surrey*, 1938, p.128.
   8. Proposal for the Great Austins Conservation Area, March 1993.
   9. *The Builders' Journal*, 27 June 1906.
   10. J.H.Elder-Duncan *Country Cottages and Weekend Homes*, p.93 describing Great Austins House.

11. *The Architects' Journal*, 19 December 1935.

4: The Small Country House and Country Cottage

1. Article by Christopher Hussey in *Country Life*, 25 November 1949.
2. See 'Edwardian Butterfly Houses' by Jill Franklin in *The Architectural Review*, April 1975.
3. Described in *Country Life*, 30 August 1919, and *Small Country Houses of Today* by R. Randall Phillips, 1925.
4. *Bumbledon*, Spring 1962 (copy in Museum of Farnham).

5: Falkner and Domestic Garden Design

This chapter quotes extensively from Falkner's letters to Betty Massingham which she incorporated into her *Gertrude Jekyll: Portrait of a Great Gardener*. Without Falkner most Jekyll biographies would be lacking good first-hand descriptions.

1. Lutyens' letter of 11 April 1897, quoted in *Letters of Edwin Lutyens to His Wife*, edited by Clayre Percy and Jane Ridley.
2. For a fuller treatment of this theme see *The English Garden and National Identity 1870-1914* by Anne Helmreich. The concept of the 'invented tradition' was first articulated by Eric Hobsbawm.
3. Interview with Alan Windsor, c.1980.
4. In fact Churchill was born on 30 November 1874, and Falkner on 28 November 1875.
5. *Looking Back* [private memoirs of E.G.Pearson], p.118.

6: Falkner and Farnham Town

1. Article by Susan Farrow and Michael Blower in *Farnham Herald*, 13 March 1987.
2. Raymond Francis *Looking for Georgian England*, p.40.
3. Quoted in Nigel Temple *Farnham Buildings and People*, p.xxi.
4. *Buildings of England: Surrey* (Pevsner Series) by Ian Nairn.
5. 1936 letter from HF to MacAlister (Secretary of RIBA).
6. Architectural Reminiscences in *The Builder*, 30 March 1945.
7. Aylwin became increasingly involved with Courage's Brewery, who retained him for other pubs in the area later.
8. Article by HF in *Bumbledon*, Spring 1961 (copy in Museum of Farnham).
9. Article by HF on Norman Shaw in *Country Life*, 15 March 1941.

7: The Dippenhall Fantasy

1. Letter in possession of George Baxter.
2. Michael Drury *Wandering Architects: in Pursuit of an Arts and Crafts Ideal*.
3. *Farnham Herald*, 21 November 1997.

8: Artist, Craftsman, Town Planner, Historian

1. Letter to *The Architects' Journal*, 12 January 1939, p.46.
2. Letter to *The Architects' Journal*, 18 April 1935.
3. Letter to *The Architects' Journal*, 15 January 1913.
4. HF letters dated 25/3/15 and 1/2/32, filed with the Norman Shaw papers at RIBA.
5. Letter to Christopher Hussey, now in Surrey History Centre Library at Woking, ref. Zs/318/1.

9: Epilogue

1. Recollection of Henry Chetwynd Stapylton in 1938.
2. Recollections by Vicky Young, *Farnham Museum Newsletter*, June 1992.
3. From *An Appreciation of Harold Falkner*, by Alfred J. Stevens, December 1963, filed with the Ewbank Smith papers in the Museum of Farnham.

Select Bibliography

Adams, Maurice B., *Modern Cottage Architecture* (London, 1904)

Anscombe, Isabelle and Gere, Charlotte, *Arts and Crafts in Britain and America* (London, 1978)

Blomfield, Reginald, *The Formal Garden in England* (London, 1892)

Brown, Jane, *Gardens of a Golden Afternoon—the Story of a Partnership: Edwin Lutyens and Gertrude Jekyll* (London, 1982)

Brown, Jane, *Lutyens and the Edwardians* (Viking/Penguin, 1996)

Budgen, Christopher, *West Surrey Architecture 1840-2000* (Heritage of Waverley, 2002)

Davey, Peter, *Arts and Crafts Architecture* (London, 1980)

Drury, Michael, *Wandering Architects: in Pursuit of an Arts and Crafts Ideal* (Stamford, 2000)

Elder-Duncan, J. H., *Country Cottages and Weekend Homes* (London, 1906)

Ewbank Smith, William, *Edwardian Farnham* (Alton, 1979)

Ewbank Smith, William, *Farnham in War and Peace* (Phillimore, 1983)

Festing, Sally, *Gertrude Jekyll* (Penguin, 1991)

Girouard, Mark, *The Victorian Country House* (Oxford, 1971)

Girouard, Mark, *Sweetness and Light: the Queen Anne Movement 1870-1900* (Oxford, 1977)

Gradidge, Roderick, *The Surrey Style* (Surrey Historic Buildings Trust, 1991)

Gradidge, Roderick, *Dream Houses: The Edwardian Ideal* (London, 1980)

Gray, A. Stuart, *Edwardian Architecture: a Biographical Dictionary* (Ware, 1988)

Jekyll, Gertrude, *Old West Surrey* (Longmans Green, 1904, republished Phillimore, 1999)

Jekyll, Gertrude and Weaver, Lawrence, *Gardens for Small Country Houses* (Country Life, 1912)

Long, Helen, *The Edwardian House* (Manchester, 1993)

Massingham, Betty, *Miss Jekyll: Portrait of a Great Gardener* (Country Life, 1966)

Munro-Faure, Alice, *William Herbert Allen 1863-1943* (Farnham Museum booklet)

Muthesius, Hermann, *Das englische Haus* (3 vols., Berlin, 1904-5); English translation *The English House* (London, 1979)

Nairn, Ian and N. Pevsner, *The Buildings of England: Surrey* (Penguin, 1962, 2nd edn, revised by Bridget Cherry, 1971)

Nevill, Ralph, *Old Cottage and Domestic Architecture in South West Surrey* (Guildford, 1891)

Otttewill, David, *The Edwardian Garden* (Yale, 1989)

Phillips, R. Randall, *Small Country Houses of Today*, Vol. III (Country Life, 1925)

Ridley, Jane, *The Architect and his Wife: a Life of Edwin Lutyens* (Chatto and Windus, 2002)

Saint, Andrew, *Richard Norman Shaw* (London, 1977)

Service, A. (ed.), *Edwardian Architecture and its Origins* (London, 1975)

Simpson, Duncan, *C.F.A. Voysey: Architect of Individuality* (London, 1979)

Smith, Caroline, *Harold Falkner* (Farnham Museum booklet)

Sparrow, W. Shaw (ed.), *The Modern Home* (London, 1905)

Summerson, Sir John, *The Turn of the Century: Architecture in Britain around 1900* (Lecture at Glasgow University, 1975)

Stamp, Gavin and Goulancourt, A., *The English House 1860-1914* (London, 1986)

Sturt, George, *The Journals of George Sturt* (ed. E.D. Mackerness, 2 vols, Cambridge, 1967)

Sturt [Bourne], George, *Change in the Village* (1955 edn, first pub. 1912)

Temple, Nigel, *Farnham Inheritance* (Farnham, Herald Press, 1956, 2nd edn 1965)

Temple, Nigel, *Farnham Buildings and People* (1963, 2nd edn 1973 Phillimore)

Tinniswood, Adrian, *The Arts and Crafts House* (London, 1999)

Verney, Sir John, *Fine Day for a Picnic* (Farnham, Herald Press, 1968)

Watkin, David, *The English Vision* (London, 1982)

Watkin, David, *Morality and Architecture Revisited* (John Murray, 2001)

Weaver, Lawrence, *Small Country Houses of Today* (Country Life, Vol. I, 1910, Vol. II, 1922)

Weaver, Lawrence, *The Country Life Book of Cottages* (Country Life, 1913, 2nd edn 1919)

Weaver, Lawrence, *Small Country Houses—Their Repair and Enlargement* (Country Life, 1914)

Wood, Jonathan, *A Portrait of Farnham* (Farnham Herald, 2003)

Index